Stand Up
for Yourself
Without Getting Fired

STAND UP
FOR YOURSELF
WITHOUT
GETTING FIRED

●

Resolve Workplace Crises Before You
Quit, Get Axed, or Sue the Bastards

●

DONNA BALLMAN

CAREER
PRESS

Pompton Plains, NJ

STAND UP FOR YOURSELF WITHOUT GETTING FIRED
EDITED BY JODI BRANDON
TYPESET BY EILEEN MUNSON
Cover design by Wes Youssi/M80 Branding
Printed in the U.S.A.

To order this title, please call toll-free 1-800-CAREER-1 (NJ and
Canada: 201-848-0310) to order using VISA or MasterCard, or for further
information on books from Career Press.

CAREER
PRESS

The Career Press, Inc.
220 West Parkway, Unit 12
Pompton Plains, NJ 07444
www.careerpress.com

Library of Congress Cataloging-in-Publication Data

Disclaimer

Oh, come on. This is written by a lawyer. You had to know there would be one. Buying and reading this book does not create an attorney-client relationship between Donna M. Ballman, PA, and you, or between Donna Ballman and you. Although this book offers scenarios that may be similar to your situation, the suggested solutions are not guaranteed to have specific results. Nothing in this book is guaranteed to prevent you from being fired. The law is constantly changing. The writer is human, and is thus prone to making the occasional error. This book has no warranty whatsoever. It offers general career advice and not specific legal advice for your situation. If a legal issue arises, speak to an attorney who handles employment law in your state. The National Employment Lawyers Association (NELA) has members throughout the country who handle employee-side issues. Their directory can be found at *www.nela.org.*

Dedication

To everyone who works for a living,
from janitor to CEO,
from intern to human resources professional.
To employment lawyers everywhere,
fighting for workers' rights against all odds.
To justice.

■ ■ ■ ■

Acknowledgments

This book would not have been possible without the hard work and assistance of many people. To Katharine Sands of the Sarah Jane Freymann Literary Agency, my wonderful agent, who listened to my ideas and helped make them better. To Tanya Earley, who did my fact-checking and kept me on the straight and narrow. If I got it right, it's thanks to Tanya. If I got it wrong, that was all me. To Raquel Suarez, who makes sure I show up when I'm supposed to and keeps things running even when I'm holed up writing. To Suzanne Lucas, Cindy Krisher Goodman, Alison Greene, and Art Schofield, without whose support and encouragement this project never would have come to fruition. To Michael Pye of Career Press, who believed in me enough to take a chance on putting my words into print. To Jodi Brandon, my excellent editor, who made sure this book was as good as it could be, and the rest of Career Press editorial and publicity staff, who worked hard to make this book a success.

And mostly to Ben, Madeline, and Amelia, for putting up with me while I disappeared into my writing. You're my inspiration and my reason for being. I love you.

Contents

ntroduction

So, you hate your job and are ready to quit. Your boss is a flaming jerkweed and you're ready to tell him off. Or layoffs are imminent. You think you're about to be fired. Maybe you think you have a lawsuit that's your ticket out of the workplace.

Stop right there.

Before you take any drastic action, or drastic action is done to you, think. Plan. Develop a strategy to deal with your workplace crisis before it blows up. Know your rights as an employee, and your responsibilities.

It's really tempting sometimes to scream "I quit!" To write a long letter to the CEO describing how your boss is incompetent or unfair. To say something that you'll regret later. Don't do it. Because everything you put in writing or say, especially around the end of your employment, can and will be held against you.

Trust me: What you think you know about your employment rights is probably dead wrong.

Maybe you have claims against the company. Maybe, if you don't have claims yet, you will. Don't blow it by failing to act strategically now. You might save your job. Maybe get the jerk fired or disciplined. At the very least, you might develop the evidence you need to take your employer or former employer to court successfully.

As an employment lawyer who has practiced employee-side employ-ment law for more than 25 years, I sometimes wish my clients could carry me around in their purse or briefcase so I could stop them before they get themselves in trouble or fired. Now they can, and so can you.

This guide is a quick reference for some of the most common questions that come up about employee rights. This book is not meant to be legal advice or cover every employment issue. When in doubt, contact an employment lawyer in your state. It's best to get answers before you act than to wait until it's too late, or you've already done something that gets you fired, or that might cost you a case.

If I can save one employee's job, or help your lawyer and you sue the bastards and win, my work here is done.

In the Beginning:

Applications, Interviews, Accepting the Job, Contracts

Can They Really Ask That on My Application?

For many employers, the employment application is the first contact they have with you as a prospective employee. What can they ask you? What does it mean? How should you answer some of those questions? Here are some areas of concern in your employment application:

Arrests/Convictions: In some states, companies aren't allowed to ask about arrests, but if they do, answer truthfully. Same with convictions. If your conviction is expunged, check the state's law where the expunction happened. In most states, if the conviction is expunged, you can honestly answer "no" to questions about arrests and convictions, with certain exceptions (such as law enforcement jobs). Precluding applicants from being hired due to an arrest or conviction might also have an adverse impact on minorities, and could be discrimination. If they ask this, get a copy of the application or make a note of the exact question and your answer.

Age, Sex, Religion, Race, National Origin, Disability, and Genetic Information: Your employer isn't supposed to ask questions that reveal a protected status. What do you do if they ask these questions? Answer truthfully, but keep a copy of the application with the inappropriate question. If you're turned down, it might give you ammunition for a discrimination claim later. If you want the job, don't make a stink about the question.

If you feel you must raise the issue, get hired, and then point it out gently after you've become a trusted employee of at least six months to a year.

Credit Information: Many employers still conduct credit checks on prospective employees. Credit checks may have an adverse impact on women and minority applicants. If you think you've been denied a job due to a credit check, you may have a discrimination claim. Your application will ask for your written permission to conduct the credit check if the employer intends to run one on you. If you don't give permission and the credit check is run anyway, the employer is violating the Fair Credit Reporting Act and possibly your state's law.

Bankruptcy: It may be legal for an employer to refuse to hire you because you had a bankruptcy. The bankruptcy is public record and will be revealed in a background check.

Workers' Compensation Claims: Even though most states make it illegal to fire you for making a workers' comp claim, few states prohibit hiring discrimination based on workers' compensation claims. Even in those states that bar workers' compensation discrimination, the claims are public record, and the employer may find out about them. Workers' comp information may well reveal the existence of a disability, so employers who use this information against applicants do so at their peril.

References and Job History: Do you list the supervisor you reported for sexual harassment? Do you list the job where you were fired for blowing the whistle on securities violations? The legal answer is yes. Omitting employment history will give an employer an excuse to fire you later, and it will probably come up in a background check. Many companies have reference checking phone numbers where HR will only give neutral references: dates of employment and job title. If the employer was a problem employer, list the neutral reference line. Or you may have a supervisor who will still say something positive. List him or her instead of the one you know will slam you.

Signature: Some sneaky employers are putting all kinds of contractual provisions into employment applications. They may ask you to waive trial by jury, or to waive your right to go to court and force you into arbitration, and the courts are allowing these provisions to stand in some states. Beware the employer that puts these provisions in applications. Your employment with them will likely be a matter of the company constantly operating in defensive mode, treating employees as the enemy.

Lying on the Application: It's tempting to lie when you are asked a difficult question on the application. Think carefully before you do this. The consequences of lying about anything, such as job history and terminations, are that, if the employer finds out you lied, even years later, they can fire you. It can also be used as a defense to a lawsuit in order to cut off your damages. The employer will say that they could have fired you because you lied, so your right to lost wages/back pay is gone.

Donna's Tips

⊃ Answer truthfully. That's the legal answer. Career advisors will tell you to carefully frame your answers or even omit information. They're not wrong, but I can't advise you to do anything but tell the truth.

⊃ You might want to hire a professional reference checking company to find out what prospective employers will say about you so you can tailor your application and interview accordingly.

⊃ Some employers (those with at least 100 employees and government contractors) are required to report race, gender, and ethnic information of all employees to the government, and some do track this information for affirmative action purposes or other legitimate reasons. They may have to ask this information on a form separate from your application, such as on a "tear sheet." However, if this is asked pre-employment, you should make note of it and keep a copy if possible.

Can They Discriminate Against Me Because of My Bankruptcy?

The Bankruptcy Code says: "No private employer may terminate the employment of, or discriminate with respect to employment against, an individual who is or has been a debtor under this title, a debtor or bankrupt under the Bankruptcy Act, or an individual associated with such debtor or bankrupt...." Seems pretty clear, huh? Ordinary mortals read the language "or discriminate with respect to employment against" to include discrimination in hiring.

The federal appellate courts, as we know, are not made up of ordinary mortals. Several appellate courts have found that this provision did not apply to discrimination in hiring. One court said, "Had Congress wished to bar private employers from discriminating against debtors in their hiring decisions, it could have done so by adding the phrase 'deny employment' to [the law] when it amended [the law] in 1994 and again in 2005."

Why the tortured logic? Well, it's at least partly Congress's fault (isn't it always?), because they put hiring in a provision about government employers. From the Bankruptcy Code:

[A] governmental unit may not deny, revoke, suspend, or refuse to renew a license, permit, charter, franchise, or other similar grant to, condition such a grant to, discriminate with respect to such a grant against, deny employment to, terminate the employment of, or discriminate with respect to employment against, a person that is or has been a debtor under this title or a bankrupt or a debtor under the Bankruptcy Act, or another person with whom such bankrupt or debtor has been associated....

These courts assume that Congress thinks like they do (Congress doesn't) and they are failing to take into account that the two provisions weren't passed at the same time.

Sure, Congress could have included that language. But congresspeople are ordinary mortals who assumed that the phrase "discriminate with respect to employment" meant what it says. These cases are popping up all over now. Maybe the Supreme Court will decide which interpretation wins out. So far, they have declined to review these cases.

In my opinion, employers who refuse to hire you just because of your bankruptcy are idiots. What on earth does that have to do with your skills? Why exclude an increasingly large number of potential candidates just because the economy tanked?

Donna's Tips

➲ If you have a bankruptcy and the employer is doing a background check, disclose it up-front. That way you don't waste your time if they consider it an automatic disqualification.

➲ Encourage your Congressperson to act to change this messed-up law.

⊃   Follow this issue closely, because it will be in flux for a while until the Supreme Court or Congress fixes it.

Wait, They Can't Discriminate Because of My Criminal Record, Can They?

Discrimination based on your criminal record is mostly legal. However, if your record was expunged, you may be legally able to answer "no" if asked whether or not you've ever been convicted of a crime. Know the law in your state. If you're arrested, you'd better understand the employment consequences before you agree to cop to a plea.

At least one state has a law making discrimination based on criminal records illegal. A few others won't allow employers to ask about arrests or convictions. Others have established commissions to possibly address discrimination against ex-offenders by employers. A couple of states have limits on whether your occupational license can be revoked/denied. Some have processes you can go through to limit disclosure of your records to employers. Most still allow employers to ask about criminal records.

Some jobs, like law enforcement, teaching, and the military, don't allow you to hide behind an expunction. If you're applying for a job, check the laws in your state to make sure you're allowed to fail to disclose a conviction.

A "no contest" or sealed conviction is still something you must disclose if asked in most states. Unless your record is expunged or sealed, it is public record, and a potential employer could uncover it in a background check.

If you fail to disclose a criminal record when asked, and you aren't allowed to say it didn't happen (as with an expunction), then the employer can fire you for failing to disclose it, even if you've worked there for years with no problems.

In my view, this issue will be ultimately addressed as one of disparate impact on minorities, like credit checks. With the disproportionate amount of African-Americans in our system, it's only a matter of time before some cases emerge saying criminal history discrimination equals race discrimination. The EEOC takes the position that blanket refusals to hire people with convictions may indeed have an adverse impact on minorities.

Right now, assume you'll have to disclose it and prepare with a career counselor on how to answer questions about a conviction in interviews and applications.

Donna's Tips

- When in doubt, tell the truth.

- Know what you were convicted of and whether or not the record was expunged. Lots of my clients have no idea the actual charges that they were convicted of. It makes a difference. If you don't care about your criminal record, many employers assume that you think committing crimes is okay.

- In a lawsuit, the lawyer from the other side is allowed to ask whether you have ever been convicted of a felony, and whether you've ever been convicted of a crime involving dishonesty. Assume the other side will find out if you're lying. It's best to tell your lawyer in advance if you have a conviction so he or she can be prepared to deal with it.

They Can't Ask That During My Interview, Can They?

Interviewers ask the darndest things. Some of it actually has to do with your ability to do the job. Some has to do with how you'll fit in with co-workers and the corporate culture. Every once in a while, they ask something inappropriate.

Here are examples of questions that may force you to disclose a legally protected status:

Arrests/Convictions: Some states don't allow interviewers to ask about arrests or convictions, but most still do. Mostly, interviewers don't ask about this. You're more likely to be asked on the application. If the interviewer does ask, then you may be able to answer "no" truthfully if your record is expunged, but probably not if it's just sealed. You should check the state where you were arrested to see how it deals with sealing and expunction. If you aren't hired and the conviction had nothing to do with your ability to do the job, you might also have potential discrimination claims. Minorities and men are definitely more adversely impacted by a blanket exclusion of people with records than women and whites, because they're statistically more likely to have a criminal history.

Age, Sex, Religion, Race, National Origin, Disability, and Genetic Information: You'd think that questions about race wouldn't come up in interviews because race is usually apparent once you're face to face. But I've actually met people who were asked flat-out: "What are you?" or "What race are you?" The interviewer isn't supposed to ask questions that reveal a protected status. If the interviewer does ask, answer truthfully.

Some examples of questions that actually do come up frequently because people are curious, no matter how well-trained they are:

❯ Where are you from? Seems harmless, but if you're from, say, Iran, the interview might turn sour quickly.

❯ What happened to you? An interviewer who sees you in a cast, on crutches, or even in a wheelchair might not be able to resist.

❯ Can you work Sundays (or Saturdays)? Why not? You might be forced to disclose your religious beliefs if you have holy days that must be accommodated.

❯ What year did you graduate high school? College? If your answer is in the 1980s, 1970s, or earlier, you can almost hear the interviewer doing math in his or her head.

❯ Why have you been out of the job market so long? In some states, it's illegal to discriminate against you because you're unemployed. This question might force you to disclose a disability, kids, marital status, domestic violence, or another protected status.

❯ Do you have any kids? How old? This is pretty normal to ask anyone in conversation, but it might reveal a recent pregnancy, maternity leave, marital status, or need for breastfeeding accommodations. The interviewer might look at women with kids differently than men with kids. He or she might start asking questions about your ability to travel, or work weekends or evenings, or how you deal with sick kids.

Lawsuits: If you're asked whether you've ever been in a lawsuit, there are all kinds of potential land mines. If you reveal a foreclosure or a bankruptcy (which isn't technically a lawsuit), you're revealing credit information. If you reveal a divorce, it's marital status. If you've sued an employer or made a workers' compensation claim, you might have to kiss the job goodbye even if they supposedly aren't allowed to retaliate against you. If you reveal a personal injury claim, you might also be revealing a disability. Questions about lawsuits are more likely to come out if there's been a background check already. Employers who ask about or look into lawsuits are asking for trouble, but that doesn't mean they won't do it anyway.

Donna's Tips

- An inappropriate question doesn't mean you've just been handed a lottery ticket. The fact of asking the question isn't enough, by itself, for you to sue. The question may, however, be evidence that the hiring decision (or later employment decision) was based on something illegal. Write it down when you get in the car or out of the building. Make a note of the question, your answer, and anyone present who heard it.

- Answer truthfully. There are ways of answering truthfully that might be better than others. If you have a protected status you are concerned about, be ready for questions like these. Practice how you will answer. Ask for advice from a career counselor or trusted advisors.

- If you did reveal your protected status and were turned down, try to find out who was hired. If you were more qualified, you might have a case.

Can My Potential Employer Make Me Take a Lie Detector Test?

Mostly, the answer is no. The Employee Polygraph Protection Act of 1988 prohibits private employers from using lie detector tests to screen potential employees or during the course of their employment, with some exceptions. It doesn't apply to government employers. Here's what you need to know about polygraphs at work:

Can't Suggest: Employers can't suggest, require, request, or cause an employee or potential employee to take a polygraph.

Can't Ask: Employers cannot inquire about, use, accept, or refer to polygraph results of employees or potential employees.

Can't Retaliate: Employers can't discriminate against employees or potential employees who refuse to take a polygraph. That means no discharge, discipline, denial of employment, or threats.

Exceptions for Potential Employment: Security firms, pharmaceutical firms that handle controlled substances, and federal contractors that handle issues of national intelligence have some limited exceptions that apply to polygraphs and to other types of lie detectors.

Prohibited Lie Detector Tests: These are polygraph, deceptograph, voice stress analyzer, psychological stress evaluator, and similar devices.

A polygraph is an instrument that records continuously, visually, permanently, and simultaneously changes in cardiovascular, respiratory and electrodermal patterns.

Exceptions: If your employer has a reasonable basis to suspect you were involved in an incident that resulted in a monetary loss to them, and if you had access to the property that is the subject of the investigation, then they can subject you to a polygraph under strict guidelines.

Even if the employer can give the polygraph, you have rights, including:

> *Written notice* explaining your rights and the limitations imposed on the testing.

> The *right to refuse* to take the test, to terminate it, or to decline to take it if you have a medical condition.

> The *right not to have the results disclosed* to anyone other than the employer or you, except by court order or to a government agency or court, an arbitrator, or mediator.

There are strict limitations on what you can be asked and how the test is to be conducted. If they violate any part of this law, you might have a legal claim against the employer.

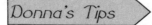

Donna's Tips

⊃ There's a reason most courts don't allow lie detector tests to be admitted: They're unreliable. False positives are common. If you're nervous, you may well fail. There's little upside to agreeing to a polygraph.

➲ Many clients say to me, "Tell them I'm willing to take a poly-graph." Too bad. The employer can't give you one even if they wanted to in most cases.

➲ If you did steal money or property from your employer, for heaven's sake, get a criminal defense lawyer. Don't take the polygraph. It's better to be fired than to go to jail. Say nothing. You have the right to remain silent, so zip it.

Can an Employer Refuse to Hire Me Because I Have Bad Credit?

If your state is like most, an employer can refuse to hire you due to bad credit. Some states finally got wise and passed laws against using poor credit history as the basis for employment decisions. If your potential employer is going to run a credit check, then they must comply with the Fair Credit Reporting Act.

A consumer report covered by the Fair Credit Reporting Act is anything the employer is getting from a consumer reporting agency that covers personal and credit characteristics, character, general reputation, or lifestyle. This doesn't cover the HR department running your name on Google, checking out your Facebook page, or reading your blog. Here's what you need to know about credit checks by employers:

Notice: They must give you a document that is solely for the purpose of telling you they intend to conduct a credit check. It was probably shoved in with a stack of papers they handed you with your application or pre-employment forms.

Written Permission: The employer needs your written permission to conduct a credit check. If you're surprised they did a credit check, you probably signed something giving permission and didn't read it. Remember when I said to read everything they stick in front of you?

Pre-Adverse Action: The employer must tell you if they're about to deny a job, reassign, or terminate you because of what was disclosed in a credit report. They must give you written notice with a copy of your credit report and a document called "A Summary of Your Rights Under the Fair Credit Reporting Act." This process does not apply to truckers.

After Adverse Action: The employer must give another notice, this time telling you the name of the agency that did the credit report, saying the agency isn't the one that made the adverse decision, and telling you how to dispute the information in the report with the agency. This notice can be verbal or in writing, unless you're a trucker, in which case it must be written.

Discriminatory Impact: The EEOC is looking closely at the use of credit reports in employment decisions because they frequently have a disparate impact on women and minorities.

Donna's Tips

- ⊃ If you have bad credit, be ready to explain your situation. Tell the interviewer your plan to address the situation. While being "in over your head" may be considered an indicator of potential dishonesty, it doesn't mean you're going to become an embezzler. If you can demonstrate that you have a plan to get out from under the debt, the HR department might feel reassured.

- ⊃ If an employer runs your credit history without permission, they've broken the law. Period.

- ⊃ If the employer doesn't jump through all the hoops required under the Fair Credit Reporting Act, you have potential claims against them.

Is My Offer Letter a Contract?

Some people say, "But I don't have a contract." When I ask them if they got an offer letter, many did. They say, "But that's not a contract, is it?" Sure, the offer letter is probably a contract. It's an offer and you accepted. There was consideration for it—namely, you started working. Those are all the basic requirements for the formation of a contract.

But what does that contract actually say? How much weight does it have? Like every other contract, it depends. Here's what you should watch out for in your offer letter:

Pay: If it lays out your pay structure in writing and says it can only be changed in writing signed by both parties, then they can't change it without your agreement. If it lays out the pay without language about modifications, then most pay plans can be unilaterally changed by the employer at any time.

At Will: If it says you can be fired at will, or if it's silent on whether or not you're at will, then in almost all states you can be fired at any time for any reason. That means they can fire you for not agreeing to change your pay terms or other key employment terms.

Cause: If it says you can only be fired for cause, then what are your remedies if you're fired without cause? If the offer says you will be employed from X date to Y date, then you should get paid out for that time period. It might say that if you're fired without cause you get a specific amount of severance. It might say that they can fire you without cause with X days of notice, in which case you get paid out for the notice period.

Conditional Offer: If the letter says it's conditional, then don't quit your job yet. If you must pass a background check, wait for written confirmation you've passed. If they tell you verbally, send them an e-mail confirming the conversation and say you're relying on their representation that you've passed. Let them know that you'll be giving notice at your job in the next X number of days unless they notify you that this is incorrect. The offer could also be conditional under the Americans with Disabilities Act. That means you will now have to disclose any accommodations you need for a disability. If they decide they can't accommodate you without undue hardship, they can pull the offer.

Donna's Tips

⊃ If you are leaving a secure job for a new position, try to get some assurances in writing about job security. If they want you badly enough, they might agree to put in that they can only terminate for cause and some reasonable severance.

⊃ If you do get a contract, be careful what you sign. I've seen unscrupulous competitors lure top salespeople, have them sign non-compete agreements, then fire them a few months later. Surprise! You're out of the industry unless you have the financial resources for a long legal fight.

⊃ Do your due diligence before you accept a job that sounds too good to be true. Google the new employer. Ask to speak to some coworkers before you accept. See if you can find some former employees (try LinkedIn, which lists former employers) to talk to about what their experiences were.

I Got the Job and Now They Want Me to Sign a Contract With a Bunch of Legal Mumbo Jumbo.
Should I Go Ahead and Sign Even If I Don't Understand It?

Never, ever sign anything without reading and understanding it first. Employers will shove a dozen documents under your nose your first day and demand you sign them. If anything is titled "Contract" or "Agreement" or even looks like a contract and you don't understand it, run—do not walk—to an employment attorney to have it reviewed.

You should understand what you're agreeing to, and assume it will be enforced. Don't sign it unless you can live with it. Here are some of the agreements you might be asked to sign before or right after you start working:

Employment Agreement: This sets out your job title, compensation, and terms of employment, and the length of the agreement. It might say you're an at-will employee, in which case you can be fired at any time for any reason. It might say you can only be fired for cause. Look at the definition of "cause" carefully. If it's up to the employer's discretion, you're still probably an at-will employee. Before you start working is the time to negotiate the terms of your employment agreement. If you have anything the employer has promised or you think is essential that's not in the agreement, you'd better get it in the agreement or it won't happen.

Confidentiality Agreement: You may be agreeing to keep the employer's confidential information to yourself, but sometimes these agreements say you won't compete with the employer for a year or two. Sometimes they say you can't invent, create, or write anything while you're employed without the employer owning it.

Non-Compete Agreement: You're maybe agreeing not to work in your industry for a year or more after you cease working for this employer. Don't sign it if you can't live with it.

Non-Solicitation Agreement: This means you won't solicit the company's customers to leave them, or their employees, to go to another company. Courts like to uphold these agreements, so understand what you're agreeing to do.

Intellectual Property Agreement: Some companies want you to agree that anything you thought of, designed, created, wrote, or conceived of while you were employed, belongs to them. This is great if you're not a creative person. But if you write novels, paint, design video games, sketch doll designs, or do anything creative, you'd better be careful what you sign. Just ask the Bratz guys. They designed the first Bratz dolls while working for Mattel. They had to litigate for years to get back the rights to their own designs.

Donna's Tips

➲ If you're presented with a contract, read it carefully. You may want to have an employment lawyer take a look if there's something you don't understand. Yes, you'll have to pay for a contract review. But it's best to understand what you're agreeing to before you sign.

➲ Don't believe anyone (except maybe a lawyer who practices employment law in your state) who tells you these agreements are never enforced. They're wrong.

➲ Failing to read or understand a contract is never an excuse to evade complying with an agreement.

➲ If you're bound by an agreement, make sure you have a copy. Some employers resist giving a copy, which I don't understand. How can an employee comply with an agreement if they don't have a copy? If your employer resists, tell them you want it to make sure you don't violate it accidentally. Hopefully, they'll give it to you. If they claim you've violated an agreement you don't have a copy of, ask for it or have your lawyer ask for a copy. Don't just believe them if they claim you've signed something. Lots of employers assume everyone has signed when they haven't.

➲ Some states allow employers to fire you if you refuse to sign a contract. Before you refuse, understand your rights in your state.

What Does It Mean That I Agree to Arbitrate?

Arbitration agreements pop up all over the place in employment situations. Some of the documents employers like to stick them in to get you to sign away your right to sue are applications, handbooks, employment agreements, arbitration agreements, union contracts—just about any place they can think of to get you to sign without thinking.

Even if you have time to think about them, most states will let employers get away with making you sign away rights you thought were guaranteed in the Constitution.

If an employer presents you with an arbitration agreement pre-employment, that's the time to negotiate to make it go away. If the employer won't negotiate, you can accept it or turn down the job. If they present it to you after you've accepted the job, most states will let them say: "Sign it or be fired."

Courts love arbitration agreements. It lightens their workload. Don't expect help from the courts anytime soon. The remedy will have to be through Congress or your state legislature.

Here's what you should know about arbitration before you agree to it:

Arbitration Defined: Arbitration is where two or more parties agree to submit their dispute to a neutral third party instead of the courts. Some arbitration is non-binding—that is, the parties can still go to court if they aren't satisfied with the decision. But most arbitration is binding. That means you don't even get to appeal an arbitrator's decision under most circumstances.

Arbitrators: An arbitrator who handles employment arbitrations is usually a current or former employment lawyer, HR person, or other individual with experience in employment law matters. Arbitrators go through training on the process before they are approved to be on a panel. Depending on your arbitration agreement, you may have one or three arbitrators. You will usually have some input into the choice of your arbitrator. You will always be able to seek to remove an arbitrator if he or she has a conflict of interest.

Rules: Most arbitration forums have detailed rules you must follow. Make sure you elect a forum, if you have a choice, that has employment rules, not just general commercial rules. Employment rules usually have some built-in due process protocols to protect individuals. Commercial rules are more geared toward businesses, and presume businesses are represented and experienced in arbitrations.

Discovery: Usually, arbitration relies on the mutual exchange of documents, no depositions, and no full discovery like you'd get in court. However, in employment situations, many arbitrators will allow limited discovery and depositions. It's important to understand what will be allowed.

Costs: Who bears the costs is decided in the arbitration agreement or, if the agreement is silent, in the rules of the arbitration forum. If the rules require the employer and employee to split costs equally from the beginning, that's a huge advantage for the employer. Remember: Arbitrators must be paid for their time. Most employees, especially unemployed ones, can't afford to pay. The better way is to have the employer bear the costs from the beginning. Then, if the employee loses, have them assessed with all or some of those costs at the end. But if your employer chose the forum and wrote the agreement, can you guess which way they'll likely choose?

Time: The good news is that arbitration is usually quicker than a court case. The bad news is that there may be shortened deadlines for filing. Read your agreement and the rules very carefully.

Donna's Tips

➲ Arbitration has lots to offer as a form of alternate dispute resolution. It can save time and money. The person making the decision is experienced in employment law. If there are due process protocols in place and a fair cost allocation, arbitration is nothing to fear.

➲ Just because a proposed arbitrator handles primarily employer-side law doesn't mean he or she will be bad on your case. Most arbitrators take their position as neutrals very seriously. I'm an arbitrator, and I've ruled for both management and employees. Go for experience and a balanced resume, and, if you can, look at some prior decisions before you make a decision on which arbitrators to strike from your panel.

➲ Sometimes both sides hate the arbitrator choices the forum offers. Both sides can agree on an arbitrator they like.

➲ Most objections you hear in court won't come up in arbitration. Arbitrators can hear irrelevant evidence, and all sorts of evidence and testimony that would be inadmissible in court. They tend to err on the side of allowing more, rather than less, information.

Crisis Scenarios for Applications, Interviews, and the First Few Days of Work

Scenario 1

You're applying for a job you really want. Your dream job—or so you thought. The application asks your sex, marital status, and ages of your children. Do you:

❑ a. Rip up the application and walk out? The questions are a really bad sign. Who wants to work for a company that would ask discriminatory questions?

❑ b. Leave the answers blank? Hopefully the interviewer will not hold it against you. Maybe they'll even know the questions are inappropriate and won't expect answers.

❑ c. Fill it out completely? Keep a copy. If you're turned down, this might be ammunition for a discrimination claim.

If you answered a:

You may be right. But why give up your dream job without getting more information? You now have zero chance of getting the job.

If you answered b:

This is not a bad choice. Sometimes skipping the inappropriate questions may be your only option. If the interviewer follows up and asks the same questions again, you'll have a choice to make about how you deal with it. On the other hand, you might not get the interview if you leave questions blank.

If you answered c:

This is the ideal option from an employment lawyer's perspective. It's evidence of discrimination if you don't get the job. If you get the job, great. Save it for later. It might be evidence of discrimination down the road.

Scenario 2

A job application has, in tiny print at the bottom, a notation that says: "Applicant agrees that any dispute relating to this application or subsequent employment with ABC Company will be submitted to arbitration under the commercial rules of the U.S. Arbitration Association. Applicant further waives the right to jury trial for any dispute related to this application or employment with ABC Company." Do you:

- ❑ a. Sign? It isn't enforceable anyway.
- ❑ b. Get the heck out of there? Don't sign. Look elsewhere for employment.
- ❑ c. Leave the signature line blank?

If you answered a:

You're wrong. Courts love to enforce stuff like this in most states. It lightens their dockets. If you need the job and have few options, go ahead and sign. Assume it will be enforced if you do.

If you answered b:

This might be your best option. If the employer is already being sneaky and underhanded, and trying to get you to waive your legal rights before you even get an interview, it's a terrible sign for how your employment would go.

If you answered c:

You might not get any further in the process. On the other hand, they might not notice, at least for a while. If you get interviewed and they ask why you didn't sign, you'll have some explaining to do. And truthfully, if you get this job, they'll probably make you sign away your rights again when you fill out the first day paperwork.

Scenario 3

You arrive your first day of work and a bunch of papers are shoved in front of you. The HR person says, "Here's your paperwork. I need it all back on my desk, signed, in 30 minutes." There's no way you have time to read everything you're being asked to sign. Do you:

- ❑ a. Say, "There's no way I can read through all this in 30 minutes. Can I get it to you by the end of the day?"

❑ b. Rush through it without reading and sign everywhere indicated? You want to make sure you don't blow the very first deadline you're given.

❑ c. Fill out what you can? At the end of 30 minutes, take what you've done to HR and say, "Here's what I have so far. I haven't had a chance to read the rest. Can I get it back to you tomorrow?"

If you answered a:

This is not a bad option. If it's obvious you aren't being given enough time, you might want to ask for more time up front. On the other hand, if she says no, you're kind of stuck.

If you answered b:

You're like most people, who don't bother reading all that stuff. You just signed papers agreeing you can't ever sue the employer, that if you're fired tomorrow you can't work for a competitor for two years, and that your compensation package was reduced to minimum wage for the probation period, which is the first year. Not to worry. Enjoy the new job!

If you answered c:

This may be your best option. Go through the fast stuff first: declaring your dependents and tax deductions, short forms, signing that you've received your handbook. Then look at the long, confusing stuff. If you understand it, sign. If you don't, then you may need to ask HR for clarification if it's not anything called "Agreement" or "Contract." If it has one of those words, you might need to take it to a lawyer to review, in which case you should ask for even more time to turn it in.

Scenario 4

Same as scenario 3, except you see a document called, "Employee Confidentiality Agreement." It's 20 pages and you can't understand a word. Do you:

❑ a. Sign it? You have no intention of giving away company confidential information. It's just a formality.

❑ b. Announce, "I'm not signing this. It wasn't part of what I agreed to when I signed the offer letter."?

❏ c. Ask what it is? When the HR person says, "It's just a formality. Don't worry. These are never enforceable anyhow," you go ahead and sign it.

❏ d. Say, "I'm going to take this to my lawyer to review it. Can I get this back to you next week?"

If you answered a:

You're like most people. Who needs to read that legal mumbo jumbo? You've probably signed away the rights to the novel you've been working on for 10 years (I'm not kidding; look at the part about inventions and copyrights), your right to work for a competitor anywhere in this solar system for two years, and your right to contact anyone in the book of business you're bringing with you (including your brother, your best friend, and your mom) after you leave the company.

If you answered b:

In most states you can be fired for refusing to sign. Hopefully you have another offer you didn't turn down yet.

If you answered c:

She's lying. Never sign anything assuming it can't be enforced. If it's never enforced, why is the company asking you to sign? Their lawyers aren't (usually) that stupid. Though it's possible that making employees sign is a way to intimidate them and keep them from trying to leave, it's more likely that the lawyers will sue you, your new employer, your mother, your dog, and everyone you ever met if they think you breached. Oh, all right. I might be exaggerating about the dog. Unless they think he knows something....

If you answered d:

In a perfect world, HR will say okay. You'll take it to a lawyer, who will explain what you're signing. If there's something horrible, maybe you can even convince the company to change some parts. In the meantime, you've bought yourself some time. Maybe another offer will come in, or maybe you send out some resumes just in case.

The First Few Weeks:

Starting Your New Job

I Don't Need to Bother Reading the Company Handbook, Do I?

In most states, your company handbook isn't a contract. That doesn't mean you don't have to pay close attention to its rules. Your employer may not have to follow their own procedures, but you do. Some employers are starting to make employees sign them and add things like an agreement to arbitrate all claims against the employer or a waiver of jury trial.

You will want to read your handbook and understand your rights and responsibilities.

Sections you should pay extra careful attention to are:

Discrimination Policy: Where do you report discrimination? Who do you report it to if your supervisor is the person discriminating? If you're a federal employee, your deadlines are extremely short, so be aware. Know your policies before you need them.

Harassment Policy: Ignore when they say to report all harassment. But do report harassment based on race, age, sex, national origin, disability, genetic information, religion, color, whistle-blowing, making a worker's comp claim, or taking Family and Medical Leave. Follow the published policy to the letter (except if it says to report verbally, make sure you also report in writing).

Sick Leave/Personal Leave: Understand who you must call and how far in advance. Don't give them an excuse to fire you.

Family and Medical Leave: The employer must publish the process you must follow to take FMLA leave. Make sure you follow all the steps and get them whatever medical certifications they require.

Donna's Tips

⊃ Knowing your handbook makes sense. These are the employer's rules and you must follow them.

⊃ Make sure you keep your copy of the handbook. If the employer wants you to sign saying you've received it but they won't let you keep it, sign, then write: "Saw briefly, not allowed to keep a copy."

⊃ Pay attention to those updates the employer sends around in memo form.

⊃ If it's a contract for one party, it's a contract for both. Be careful what you sign. If your company wants you to sign away your rights, have a lawyer take a look or make sure you understand what you're agreeing to.

⊃ If the company fails to follow their own policies, that might be evidence of discrimination or retaliation if they follow the policies for other employees.

I Started and Found Out I Have No Benefits. Don't They Have to Provide Benefits?

I sometimes have people tell me they started their new job and then found out there was no health insurance. They express shock: *But they have to give me insurance, don't they?*

No, they don't. There is no federal law requiring any employer to provide any particular benefits to employees. There are some tax incentives for employers to provide benefits such as health insurance and 401(k) plans, which is why so many do (that, and the executives want them). Also, some large businesses must pay an assessment if they don't provide health insurance. Some states do have health insurance requirements, but they are a small minority.

You should always ask about benefits before you accept a new job. The time to negotiate is before you accept, not after you start.

Even though employers don't have to provide benefits, once they do, the benefits are regulated by law. Here are some things you should know about benefits you might get in your new job, what happens to your benefits when you leave, and the federal laws that govern benefits:

ERISA: The Employee Retirement Income Security Act of 1974 (ERISA) is a federal law that sets minimum standards for most voluntarily established pension and health plans in private industry (not government entities or churches). ERISA requires your employer to provide you with plan information (theoretically in plain English—ha!) that explains your benefits. It also requires your employer to set up a grievance and appeals process if your benefits are denied. Don't lose it or toss those boring Summary Plan Descriptions and other documents your employer or plan administrator sends when you start. You'll need them if you have any questions, and the employer must follow them to the letter.

Health Insurance: Read up on your new coverage to make sure you get enrolled as soon as you qualify so you don't get stuck with high COBRA premiums any longer than you must. The Consolidated Omnibus Budget Reconciliation Act (COBRA) gives your family and you the right to choose to continue your health insurance if you lose it due to job loss, reduced hours, death, divorce, or other life events. COBRA applies to employers with 20 or more employees, and some states have statutes covering smaller employers. The employer has 30 days after you're terminated or another qualifying event to notify the plan administrator. (If the "qualifying event" is divorce or separation, you must notify the administrator within 60 days.) The administrator must send all plan participants and beneficiaries an election notice within 14 days after it gets notice of a qualifying event. You'll have 60 days to make your election to continue your coverage, and 45 days after you elect coverage to pay your first premium. It's wildly expensive. Still, nothing will bankrupt you faster than unexpected hospital bills, so elect it if you can.

401(k): If your new employer has a 401(k) plan, you'll get to roll any vested benefits over from your old plan. To the extent your former employer provided matching funds, look at your vesting schedule. If your matching funds weren't vested, you may have lost them when you left. You'll want to get the paperwork for your rollover as soon as you're eligible to participate in the new 401(k).

Life and Disability Insurance: If your former employer provided life or disability insurance, you probably lost this when you left. Some insurance companies will allow you to purchase continuation coverage, but they don't have to. It's important to find out if and when you'll qualify to enroll in your new insurance plans. There may be a limited time to enroll.

Pension: Few employers provide true pension plans anymore. If you do have a pension plan, ERISA covers it. You should look at your Summary Plan Description (remember how I told you not to lose it?) to understand when you can elect your pension, what circumstances cause you to forfeit it, and the benefits you'll get at each age you may elect. It's important to understand your pension benefits when you start and when you are getting ready to leave.

Vacation: Employers don't have to offer paid vacation (or any vacation). However, if they do, then they must let you use it if you take Family and Medical Leave. If you quit or are fired, you may, under some circumstances, be entitled to have your accrued vacation paid out. If the employer has a "use it or use it" policy, you won't get your vacation paid out. Most employers only allow you to roll over some vacation from the prior year, or require you to use it by the end of the year or lose it. Vacation is sometimes considered an "Employee Welfare Benefit Plan" under ERISA, and then it must be paid out when you leave. The vacation policy should be in your new handbook. Read it and understand it.

Severance: No law requires severance to be paid. However, if an employer has a published severance policy, it is probably an "Employee Welfare Benefit Plan" under ERISA and it must be followed. Employment contracts may also provide for severance. Read your handbook to see what your rights are if you're terminated.

Contract: If you have an employment agreement, make sure your benefits are set out in the agreement, including what happens to them when you leave.

Handbook: Read your handbook. Know your benefits and your rights under all benefits plans. Take it and keep it at home, or at least make a copy if you can. If you are terminated, it's an important document to have, and it's handy if you have a medical emergency that keeps you out of the office.

Donna's Tips

○ Just because you have a certain number of days of sick leave, that doesn't mean you should use it all. I've seen people fired for poor attendance even if they had sick time left.

○ Make sure you understand your benefits and how they work. You have responsibilities regarding your benefits, and if you don't jump through every hoop and deadline, you might lose important benefits.

The Company Wants Me to Sign a Paper Saying I'm a Contractor, Not an Employee. What Does That Mean?

Many employers try to save money on taxes and escape liability under employment laws by getting employees to sign independent contractor agreements. There are some advantages to being an independent contractor, but most people labeled as contractors are really employees. Here's what you should know if presented with an Independent Contractor Agreement:

Intellectual Property: If you are creating art, written work, computer programs, or other creative works, then it may be an advantage to you to be a contractor. Generally, you own the copyright to works created as a contractor. However, be very careful. If the contract says the work you are creating belongs to the company, you are probably giving up one of the main advantages to being a contractor.

Taxes: As a contractor, you'll pay both halves of your Social Security and Medicare taxes. If you're an employee, the employer pays half. This is a big chunk of pay to give up, so be sure you're really a contractor before you sign. The good news is that the IRS takes a dim view of employees misclassified as contractors. There's even a form (SS-8) to fill out if you think you're misclassified, to make your employer to pay what they owe.

Control: If you perform services for someone and they control what you do and how you do it, you're probably an employee. An employer controls the time, place, and manner of your work. That means if they watch your hours, make you come in the office, make you ask permission to take time off, or supervise your assignments, you may be an employee. Contractors do the work where, when, and how they choose. Nobody tells them what order to do the job in, what hours to work, or when they can take off.

Equipment and Supplies: Do they tell you what equipment to use? Where to buy it? Do they provide a desk, computer, or tools? If so, that's a good indication that you're an employee. Contractors generally use their own equipment and supplies.

Assistants: If you are told who will assist you and can't choose your own assistants, you may be an employee. Contractors can usually hire their own assistants, or choose to work alone.

Evaluations: If you are evaluated about the process, details, and methods of your work, you may be an employee. An independent contractor is evaluated on results—the end product, not the procedures used.

Training: If the company trains you on how they want the job done and the specific procedures to be used, you're probably an employee. Training for independent contractors should be minimal; only instruction on the overall results is needed.

Financial Control: Employers will reimburse many expenses, whereas contractors may have to purchase their own equipment. Pay for employees is normally done by the hour, day, or week. Contractors are more frequently paid by the job, although are sometimes paid hourly. Contractors have more opportunity to make a profit or take a loss than an employee.

Opportunity to Work Elsewhere: Contractors frequently advertise and are free to take work from other companies. Employees usually must work for a single employer only. If you want to be a consultant, free to work for many companies, then you're probably best off as a contractor.

Benefits: If the company provides insurance, sick days, vacation time, pension, or other benefits, then you are likely an employee.

Indefinite Time: If you are hired for an indefinite period of time, as opposed to working on a specific project or series of projects, then you may be an employee.

Donna's Tips

⊃   There is no one factor that will determine that you're an employee. The IRS and the courts weigh all the factors and look at the total picture of your employment. If you think you are misclassified, you do have options. Just because you signed an agreement saying you were a contractor doesn't necessarily make it so. You can talk to the employer about it if you still work there. You can also fill out that IRS form and see what happens. If you are fired for objecting to being misclassified, you may be protected from retaliation as a whistle-blower.

⊃ Whether or not you are an employee affects your rights under discrimination, wage, hour, overtime, copyright, Family and Medical Leave, and other employment laws. It also affects you in the wallet, in the form of taxes, Social Security, Medicare, and benefits.

⊃ If you've left a company and think you might have some rights as an employee, you will want to figure out what your status really was, either through the IRS, through your own research, or with the assistance of a lawyer in your state.

⊃ Some specific independent contractors are still considered employees by the IRS. They're called "statutory employees" and include some drivers, life insurance agents, people who work from home on materials or goods, and traveling sales-people. Check with the IRS if you think you might fit into one of these categories for details.

I Quit My Old Job, Then the Job They Offered Didn't Exist or Wasn't What They Promised.

If you've been lured into a job with promises of higher pay, better title, or specific hours or location, and it turns out that the representations made to lure you in weren't true, you might have a case for fraud. Worse, sometimes people are duped into giving notice at their job, only to have the offer pulled or find out the job is nonexistent.

You may claim fraud if the statements were false, the company knew they were false or were recklessly indifferent as to their truth or falsity, they made the statement for the purpose of having you act in reliance on it, and you relied on the false statements and changed your position.

Another theory you might pursue against these unscrupulous employ-ers is tortious interference with your employment relationship. I haven't seen any cases successfully bringing this type of claim (cases in a few states say once you voluntarily leave your job there's no tortious interference), but it might be viable in your state. Basically, the theory is that the phony employer interfered with your employment, knowing that you would lose your job, and that they were reckless or negligent in their behavior.

The sad truth is that, with at-will employment, you could work one day and they could decide you were a "poor performer" or "didn't fit in." Switching jobs is a high-risk activity. Be careful out there. Do your due diligence on the new employer. See if they make a habit of this type of behavior. Try to find out what kind of turnover they have. Speak to current or former employees if you can.

In my view, doing this to someone should be a crime. In this anti-employee environment, I suspect it won't happen. Still, anyone who convinces someone to leave his or her job in this economy with pie-in-the-sky promises that turn out to be phony deserves to spend some time behind bars.

Donna's Tips

- ⊃   Get that job offer in writing. Make sure you have everything you think is essential in it. If the recruiter told you that you'd only work Monday to Thursday and you need Fridays off for a class, either make sure they put it in writing or write them a letter or e-mail confirming it.

- ⊃   If the job offer is contingent, don't give notice unless all the contingencies have been met. If you must pass a background check, wait until they tell you that you've passed, and then confirm it in writing. Tell them you're relying on that information and will be giving notice at your current job.

- ⊃   Don't move without getting some guarantees that the job will last for a minimum period. It's best to have a contract saying you can only be fired for cause if you're uprooting your family.

Can My Employer Really Say I Can't Smoke?

Most states, and some cities and local governments, have laws requiring employers to ban smoking in the workplace. That's because allergies to smoke are protected under the Americans with Disabilities Act. However, quite a few states prohibit discrimination against smokers for their off-duty smoking. Smoking is not considered a protected addiction under the Americans with Disabilities Act.

Some of the restrictions your employer might impose are:

Limiting Smoker Breaks to Lunch and Regular Breaks: This is almost certainly legal. Constant smoking breaks are disruptive and cause the employer to lose hours you're actually working.

Having a Smoking Area: This is definitely legal. The employer has a right, and very possibly a duty, to keep smoke away from employees and customers who may be allergic or have breathing issues.

Different Breaks for Smokers and Non-Smokers: This is legal, for the same reasons as having a smoking area are.

Smoking Ban on Premises: This is also legal. Many states require this, and some companies don't want to deal with the risks of exposure to those who are smoke-sensitive.

Carbon Monoxide or Nicotine Testing: Some employers have implemented these policies and have successfully fended off legal challenges. At least one tobacco-growing state has a law banning nicotine testing. Other states bar discrimination against smokers without specifically banning testing. Employers that implement these tests may be doing "medical testing" that might be covered under the Americans with Disabilities Act, HIPAA, and other health privacy laws.

Ban on Hiring Smokers: This is illegal in some states, but not all. Some states prohibit policies or hiring practices that limit off-duty smoking. Although a majority of states limit or ban discrimination based on legal off-duty smoking away from the employer's premises, there may be some exceptions in your state law for professions such as firefighters.

Incentives to Quit Smoking: Health insurance surcharges for smokers or discounts for non-smokers are increasingly used to encourage workers to quit smoking. No state law bans these incentives, so they are probably going to continue to be legal.

Donna's Tips

⊃   So far the courts have rejected challenges to smoking bans based on privacy and disability discrimination. Just because it's an invasion of your privacy doesn't mean you're protected under the Constitution.

⊃ Assume your company's policy is enforceable. Don't ignore it and think no court would uphold it. That's a good way to lose your job.

⊃ The trend seems to be that smokers are losing protections rather than gaining. Keep an eye on your state laws to see if any smoker protections have passed or are introduced. Otherwise, you're probably not legally protected as a smoker.

⊃ Smoking is bad for employers' bottom lines because smokers have higher healthcare costs and absenteeism. Expect employers to continue to push for the right to limit smoking.

⊃ If your employer tests for nicotine or carbon monoxide, you might want to contact an employment lawyer in your state to see if they are complying with medical privacy laws and the ADA.

⊃ Some states prohibit retaliation against workers who assist or demand enforcement of anti-smoking laws.

Do I Have to Join a Union?

The majority of states allow unions to have an agency shop; that is, you must pay union dues in order to work there. But some states are "right to work." That means you can work anywhere in that state, even a unionized workplace, without being forced to pay union dues. You can't actually be forced to join the union, but if you have to pay the dues, you may as well be a member.

Some unions are allowed to have closed shops, which means the employer can't hire anyone not a union member, even in right-to-work states. Airline and railway unions are exempt from right-to-work laws and the federal law making closed shops generally illegal.

My best recommendation is that if you have a union in the workplace, join it. If you don't join the union, you lose some rights you would have as a union member. Here are some issues to consider before you decide whether joining a union is right for you:

Covered Under the Agreement: Whether or not you join the union or pay dues, you are covered under the collective bargaining agreement, like it or not. That means you can't bargain for yourself outside the union, can't form a competing union, and can't go outside the grievance processes they've set out.

Say in the Agreement: If you don't join the union, you have zero say in the collective bargaining agreement. You don't get to vote on it or attend meetings to express your opinion about it.

Representation: You have the right to be represented in grievances by the union whether or not you're a member. Still, I see many cases where non-members feel they have been denied representation or had their grievances ignored.

Representative: You can't be a union representative unless you join the union.

Benefits: You are entitled to any benefits the union has negotiated with the employer.

Members-Only Benefits: You are not entitled to members only benefits. Sometimes unions get discounted rates or special deals on benefits for their members.

Elections or Meetings: You will not be allowed to participate in union elections or meetings if you are not a member.

Dues: If you're not in a right-to-work state, you might have to pay union dues. However, you cannot be forced to pay that portion of dues that go toward political activities.

Donna's Tips

- ○ If you are unhappy with your union, don't drop out. Get involved. Attend meetings. Speak up. Run to be a representative. You can't change things from the outside.

- ○ If you feel the union is not representing you properly, you may have an unfair labor practice claim you can file through the National Labor Relations Board or your state equivalent.

- ○ Right-to-work laws generally benefit employers more than employees. States with right-to-work laws tend to have lower average wages and benefits than states that allow agency shops. If your state tries to pass a right-to-work law, pay attention and be fully informed about the upsides and downsides before you vote. And vote! Don't let the appealing name fool you; these laws don't affect your employer's right to fire you at-will, or your employer's right to make you sign a non-compete agreement.

⊃   There have been attempts to pass a national right-to-work law, so pay attention to what's happening and vote accordingly.

I Have a Concealed Weapons Permit. Can I Get Fired for Having My Weapon in My Car?

Even though your employer must maintain a safe workplace, and even though something like 77 percent of all workplace homicides are committed with firearms (according to *www.bradycampaign.org/stategunlaws/publicplaces/GITW*), more and more states are passing laws that you can't be fired for having a gun in your vehicle or saying you have one. That's good for you if you're a gun owner and very bad if you've been threatened by a coworker.

While the laws vary by state, there are some common themes:

Permit: The take-your-guns-to-work laws all require that you be allowed to have the gun. Whether that means a concealed weapons permit, legal ownership, proper registration, or just that you're not prohibited from having it varies.

Locked: The weapon must be secured. The law may require the vehicle to be locked or even that the gun be in a locked container.

Personal Vehicle: The employer can almost always ban weaponry in employer-owned vehicles.

Exemptions: The laws have varying exemptions, such as if other laws would be violated by allowing them (the employer is near a school, for instance), secured parking areas, or certain types of employers (such as childcare centers). If you plan to bring your gun to work, make sure your employer isn't exempt.

Policies Banning Weapons: The laws prohibit employers from having any rules or policies banning guns in company parking lots. Some go as far as prohibiting the employer from asking if you have a weapon or searching vehicles for weapons.

Private Right of Action: The laws give aggrieved employees the right to sue employers who violate the law.

Immune Employers: Employers may be immune under these laws from liability if a coworker goes postal and grabs his or her weapon out of the car. You may not be able to say they were negligent in allowing guns at work when the laws say they must.

> *Donna's Tips*

⊃ If you are bringing a gun to work, review your employer's policies carefully. If you think the policy violates the law, go to HR with a copy of the law and discuss it with them before you bring the gun.

⊃ If you bring your gun to work, make sure you comply with the letter of the law on how to secure it, where you must park, and any required permits.

⊃ If you have a hot temper, please don't bring your gun to work. Seriously.

⊃ If someone threatens you—even if they just say in a menacing tone, "You know, I have a gun in my car"—report it to HR. If nobody is around, call the police. I don't care if it's legal for the person to have the weapon; don't play around when your safety is at risk.

Is the Company Allowed to Record All Employee Phone Calls?

Many employers record employee phone calls, but I'd wager most are breaking the law. The Electronic Communications Privacy Act is the federal law regulating how phone calls can be monitored, and most states have their own laws on this. If you find out your employer is recording or listening in on your calls, you may have some legal claims. Here's what you should know:

One-Party vs. Two-Party Consent: If you live in a one-party consent state (the majority), then only one party to a conversation needs to consent to being recorded. In a two-party (better named as "all party") consent state, every person participating in the conversation must agree to be recorded. That means customers also must be told and agree to the recording. If you signed your handbook saying you agreed to its provisions and there's a monitoring section in there, you might have consented. You may also give "implied consent" if the employer has a published monitoring policy in the handbook, on bulletin boards, or in an agreement given to employees that is well-known and consistently enforced. If you consented, you lose your right to object (although it may still be illegal to record customers, vendors, and others without their consent).

Business Extension Exemption: If the equipment is regular phone equipment provided for business use (such as phone extensions) and monitoring is for purposes of customer service or training, recording or listening may be legal even without consent. However, they are supposed to stop listening if it is clear the conversation is personal.

No Criminal or Tortious Intent: If you are being recorded for sexual harassment purposes, blackmail, or another illegal purpose, the monitoring is illegal.

Concerted Activities: The employer cannot monitor employees who are engaging in activities to discuss workplace conditions or to improve working conditions. Though this generally applies to union activities, it also means the employer can't listen in on your group of employees while you're drafting a memorandum to HR about the boss's racial harassment, as an example.

911: If you're a 911 operator, or if you call 911, your calls can and will be recorded on the 911 and other police emergency lines.

Donna's Tips

- ⊃ Employers who get this wrong face employee lawsuits, criminal penalties, jail time, and even (gasp!) disconnection of their phone service.

- ⊃ The laws are complicated about what equipment can be used for monitoring, so if you're being recorded you might want to contact the FCC or an attorney who handles electronic privacy.

- ⊃ If the employer is violating the law, you might also have tort claims for privacy or intrusion on your right of seclusion (basically the same thing) as well as federal and state statutory claims.

- ⊃ Many employers forget to check the state laws on recording or monitoring. Just because they've complied with federal law doesn't mean your state doesn't have some rules they are violating.

How Does Being on Probation Affect My Rights?

Many employers have a "probationary" period where the employee handbook or a contract says you have 30, 60, or more days of time to prove yourself and that, during that time, you're on "probation." They say they can fire you for any reason during this time. What the heck does that mean? Do you have any rights while you're on probation at work? Of course you do. Here's what you need to know about your legal rights during your probationary period at work:

Legal Protections: Not a single federal employment statute affecting your legal rights deals with "probation" periods. That means you have protection regarding discrimination, unpaid wages, minimum wage, overtime, whistle-blowing, and discriminatory harassment. If you are lucky enough to live in Montana, the only state with a law prohibiting termination without just cause, you can be terminated during the first six months, for any reason.

At-Will: Unless your contract says that, after your probation period is over, you can only be fired for cause, then you can be fired for any reason or no reason at all even after your probation is up. I've had people contact me in shock because they were fired a week after their probation ended. "But my probation was up!" they cry. "Don't they need to have cause now?" Nope. Sorry.

Unemployment: Your state probably requires you to work a minimum time period in order to qualify for unemployment. However, your previous job might count.

Benefits: Employers can establish a waiting period for benefits such as health insurance and 401(k)s.

Evidence: Probation is frequently used as evidence in discrimination or other cases, and judges and juries do tend to give this some weight. If you're on probation when you're fired, they might buy the argument that the employer had the right to do it.

Donna's Tips

- ⊃ Mostly, probation is used to remind the supervisors and HR to monitor your progress. It's not for your benefit.
- ⊃ You have the same legal rights whether or not you're on probation, but that doesn't mean you should start squawking about working conditions your first week. Unless something serious happens, like a sexual proposition, severe racial remarks, or being asked to participate in Medicaid fraud, lay low and do your work while you're on probation.

⊃   Don't slack off just because you're off probation. You can still
    be fired after probation without any reason, unless you have a
    contract saying otherwise or you live in Montana.

Crisis Scenarios for Your New Job Issues

Scenario 1

The HR person tosses a handbook on the desk along with a sheet of paper
for you to sign saying that you've read, understood, and agree with it. Do
you:

❑ a. Sign without reading? You don't want to cause trouble your
     first week.

❑ b. Pick up the handbook, start reading, and tell the HR
     representative you'll sign as soon as you've read it?

❑ c. Tell the HR representative they can't make you sign
     anything until your lawyer looks at it?

If you answered a:

You probably just agreed to arbitrate any claims you may have against
your employer. You might also have agreed to waive your right to a
jury trial for any claims, or to change the terms of your written contract. You still have no idea what your vacation policy is, how to report
sick leave, or where to report discrimination. You're fine as long as
nothing ever goes wrong the entire time you're employed.

If you answered b:

You did the smart thing. Never sign saying you've read something you
haven't. If you sign, you will be expected to know and understand the
handbook. Make sure you keep a copy of the handbook handy if you
can.

If you answered c:

You've gotten off on a bad foot. You probably don't need a lawyer for
this. However, if you see anything weird or that you don't understand,
you might want to have a lawyer look at it first. You don't need to tell
HR you're seeing a lawyer though. Why get labeled as a troublemaker
your first week?

Scenario 2

Same as scenario 1, except the HR person waves the handbook in front of you and says, "Here's the handbook. We don't let employees keep it. I have it in my office if you ever need it. Sign here." Do you:

❑ a. Say, "You've got to be kidding me. I have a right to a copy of my handbook."?

❑ b. Say, "I can't sign something saying I've read it if I haven't. Please leave it here, and I'll read it and return it to you."?

❑ c. Sign (you don't want to make trouble your first week)?

❑ d. Sign with this notation: "Not permitted to read handbook or to have copy."?

If you answered a:

You have no right to the handbook. While it's really stupid business practice to have a handbook nobody reads, there's no law requiring them to give it to you. You are on your way to being fired for insubordination.

If you answered b:

This is what I'd suggest as your first step. If the HR rep insists you sign, go for answer d. If you do have a chance to review it, take good notes. If you can, discreetly make a copy.

If you answered c:

You still have no idea what any of your rights or responsibilities are. How do you call in sick? Do you have paid time off (PTO)? What is the vacation policy? Good luck guessing.

If you answered d:

When HR digs in their heels, this may be your only option. They'll start looking at you with suspicion afterward, but it's better than signing that you've read something you never saw. I'd start looking for another job if I were you. This is not a good sign.

Scenario 3

You stand up and grab your pack of cigarettes. You head to the break room and light up. A coworker tells you that you can't smoke there. Do you:

❑ a. Apologize and ask if there's a smoking area?

❑ b. Tell the coworker to mind his or her own business?

❑ c. Report the coworker to HR for harassment?

If you answered a:

You did exactly right. Many workplaces are smoke-free. Some are smoke-free by law. They might have designated smoking areas or a safe place for smoking outside.

If you answered b:

Don't be surprised when the coworker runs to HR. If you fill the break room with smoke, the company may be violating a clean air law, so expect to be written up. Your coworker will hate you from that day forward, along with all of his or her friends.

If you answered c:

Not only have you made an enemy for life, but you got it wrong. There's no law against harassing people for smoking, and there's probably a law you're violating by smoking inside. Plus, you might be hurting someone who is allergic to smoke, has asthma, or has another breathing disorder.

Scenario 4

Same as scenario 3, except the HR person says, "I'm sorry, but we have a policy against hiring smokers. We have to let you go." Do you:

❑ a. Ask why you weren't informed of the policy when you applied?

❑ b. Tell them they'll be hearing from your lawyer?

❑ c. Refuse to leave? Tell them you know your rights and they can't fire you for smoking.

❑ d. Tell them you're an addict and you want a reasonable accommodation under the Americans with Disabilities Act?

If you answered a:

Good question. If you have a contract saying you can only be fired for cause and smoking isn't in there, you might have some rights. If you live in a state making this kind of policy illegal, you may have some legal rights. If they answer, write down the answer and take it to a lawyer.

If you answered b:

> In a majority of states, you're probably right. It might be better to leave quietly and consult a lawyer rather than to make threats.

If you answered c:

> You're probably being placed under arrest for trespassing or getting hauled out by a security guard. Do not pass go; do not collect $200. Don't be an idiot. Leave if they tell you to.

If you answered d:

> Sorry. Smoking addiction is not covered under ADA. You may have rights under state law to smoke on your own time, just not at work.

Scenario 5

You assumed that your new employer would carry health insurance. Much to your shock, you find out after you start that they don't. Do you:

- ❑ a. Barge into HR and demand your health insurance? They must cover you!

- ❑ b. Smack yourself in the forehead, chastise yourself for not asking before you accepted the job, and make sure you pay your COBRA premiums on time?

- ❑ c. Start looking for private insurance?

If you answered a:

> You'd better live in one of the few states that actually do require that employers provide insurance, and you'd better make sure they aren't exempt from this requirement. Even if you're right, it would be better to quietly provide HR with a copy of the law requiring coverage and ask them to take care of it.

If you answered b:

> This is probably your best bet. COBRA is crazy expensive, but it's better than going without coverage. Health problems are the quickest way to go bankrupt if you aren't covered.

If you answered c:

> Hopefully you're already doing b. You want to make sure you're continuously covered. But yes, to avoid the high COBRA payments, it will be best to find private coverage ASAP.

Scenario 6

You're presented with an "Independent Contractor Agreement" your first week. It says that you agree you're not an employee and you are responsible for your own taxes. Do you:

- ❏ a. Read it carefully? If there's anything you don't understand, contact a lawyer or your accountant, especially to understand the tax consequences.
- ❏ b. Sign? Whatever—hey, at least you have a job.
- ❏ c. Sign, then file a form SS-8 with IRS to have them determine whether or not you are really a contractor?

If you answered a:

This is a good option. You'll still have to decide what to do if the lawyer or accountant says you shouldn't sign. You should strategize, which might include showing them the IRS guidelines about independent contractors and some articles about how they're cracking down on employers who misclassify.

If you answered b:

You will be stuck with paying your employer's half of employment taxes. You'll have no unemployment insurance and probably no benefits. No paid vacation or sick time. On the other hand, you might be free to work for other companies as well.

If you answered c:

This is not a bad choice, although the contract is evidence of your intent to be a contractor, and the IRS will consider it in making its determination.

Scenario 7

Same as scenario 6, except you have your own company and it was always your understanding that you could work for other companies, hire your own people, and come and go as you please. Do you:

- ❏ a. Sign without reading it? Sure, this is what you expected.
- ❏ b. Read it carefully and sign only after you understand what they are having you agree to?
- ❏ c. Not bother? You don't work for them. You don't have to sign anything.

If you answered a:

You probably just gave away your rights to anything you create while you're there. You might have agreed not to work for a competitor while you're there, or even for two years after you leave. Never sign anything without reading.

If you answered b:

You're a smart businessperson. You'll probably do well.

If you answered c:

You better start looking for other companies to work for. They have the right to get your relationship on paper.

Scenario 8

You get a dream job offer by e-mail. Hooray! You quit your job, pack up your family, move across the country, and arrive by your start date. You walk in the first day and nobody knows who you are. When you finally track down the person who wrote the e-mail, they say, "Sorry. I thought we were going to have an opening, but we don't." Do you:

❏ a. Go home, get out your gun, go back, and start shooting?

❏ b. Contact a lawyer? You might have a fraud claim or other claim against the company.

❏ c. Take the e-mail to HR at the company, explain the situation, and see what they can do?

If you answered a:

I understand the temptation, truly. This was egregious. Still, you won't do your family any good in jail. It might be legal to take your gun to work and leave it in your car, but it's not legal to shoot your coworkers. The he-needed-killing defense isn't actually legally recognized—at least, not yet. It's best to get a contract specifying all terms of the new employment and a specific time period you're guaranteed not to be fired without cause if you're moving your family and leaving a steady job.

If you answered b:

You might well have some claims here. You should talk to lawyers in your old state and the state where the new company is located. You could have claims under either state's laws.

If you answered c:

It's possible HR will realize that they must take care of you in some way. If they don't take care of it, go back to answer b.

Scenario 9

You quit your job for a job that is a better title and seems in every way to be a better opportunity. When you start, they tell you that you're a "trainee" and will be able to work your way into that position, but you must work at much lower wages for six months while you train. Even then, the new position isn't guaranteed. Do you:

❑ a. Take the trainee position grudgingly, try to prove yourself, and live off your savings in the meantime?

❑ b. Contact your old job and tell them things didn't work out? See if they'll take you back.

❑ c. Contact a lawyer? You might have claims against these jerks.

If you answered a:

This may be your only option if a lawyer tells you that you don't have any claims. And it's something you can do to make money while you're exploring your options. The best thing to do is get a contract before you leave your old job that sets out job title, duties, pay, and any guarantees you have of length of employment.

If you answered b:

People sometimes don't think of this. It's smart. Many employers will be glad to have a good employee back. You might have to prove to them you intend to stay this time, but going back is often a great option if you can do it.

If you answered c:

You might have some claims, especially if the promises they made are in writing.

Scenario 10

On your first day a guy comes over and hands you a form. He says this is a union shop and you must pay your dues. You can join or not join, but everyone must pay. Do you:

❑ a. Refuse? You know you live in a right-to-work state.

❑ b. Pay but don't join? Unions are a waste. They don't actually help their members.

❑ c. Join the union and get involved?

If you answered a:

Hopefully you're right. In a right-to-work state, you do not have to pay union dues to work, unless you work for an airline or in the railroad industry. You will miss out on union benefits, but they still must represent you in grievances and some workplace issues, and you're bound by the collective bargaining agreement.

If you answered b:

If you don't live in a right-to-work state, or if you work for an airline or railroad, you might have to pay dues. You won't be able to be a union rep, won't get a say in the contract negotiations, and you will be treated like a second-class citizen by the union folks, but you are within your rights not to join.

If you answered c:

Smart move. You will have a say in the next contract, can become active, and change things from within, and you will get some benefits that unions only offer to members.

Scenario 11

You are robbed at gunpoint at work. You want to bring your gun to work from that point forward. Do you:

❑ a. Bring a registered weapon? Keep it in a lockbox in your car, but never take it inside.

❑ b. Strap on a holster and carry it? You know your Second Amendment rights.

❑ c. Contact HR about its policies on weapons at work and comply with their rules?

If you answered a:

If you live in a state that allows you to bring your gun to work, you're probably in compliance and can't be fired. However, many states still don't have this law. Each state's requirements are a little different, so you're better off double-checking before you bring it.

If you answered b:

You're probably fired. You might be arrested. Most workplaces do not allow you to carry a weapon on their premises.

If you answered c:

This is a good idea before you do anything with weapons. If they say no weapons are allowed, even in the parking lot, check your state law. Some employers allow weapons at work. I shop at a Western-wear and feed supply shop where the cashier wears a gun on her hip (probably more for show than actual use). It's not unheard of for employers to allow guns, especially in unsafe areas.

Scenario 12

You hear a suspicious beep on the phone line. When you ask about it, a coworker whispers that she knows the boss records all phone calls. Do you:

❏ a. Check the handbook and anything you signed to see if you agreed to this?

❏ b. Check to see whether you live in a one-party consent state or if your state requires that all parties to a phone call consent?

❏ c. Call the police? You're being wiretapped!

If you answered a:

This is a good first step. You might have agreed to it. If you live in a one-party consent state, your agreement is all they need to record calls you have with anyone.

If you answered b:

If you live in an all-party consent state, then they may be violating the law even if you did agree to this. They may still be allowed to record under very limited circumstances for training, customer service, or the like, so if you think they're breaking the law, it might be time to go to an attorney to find out about your rights.

If you answered c:

You'd better be right. If you are right, you may be a protected whistle-blower. If you're wrong and the recording is legal, you best look for another job.

Scenario 13

Same as scenario 12, except you find out the employer has a recorder set up at the front desk monitoring all employee conversations. Do you:

❑ a. Check to see if you signed anything consenting to this?

❑ b. Find a new job? That's creepy and illegal.

❑ c. Contact the police or a lawyer about your rights?

If you answered a:

If all employees consented, this might be legal, but it's doubtful. If they are listening in on personal conversations or conversations about working conditions, it's almost certainly illegal.

If you answered b:

That's what I'd do. In the meantime, try c.

If you answered c:

This is almost certainly illegal. You should take some steps to make sure, and then pursue either civil or criminal legal claims against them. You might want to find another job before you take legal action, even if you might be a protected whistle-blower.

Scenario 14

You are on probation at work your first 90 days. The company has a policy that it doesn't pay overtime while you're on probation, even though you're working 50 hours/week. Do you:

❑ a. Keep track of and report all your hours correctly?

❑ b. Accept the lower pay? You have no rights when you're on probation.

❑ c. Contact the Department of Labor and report them?

If you answered a:

Definitely keep good time records. They must pay you for all hours worked, and overtime for hours worked over 40 hours/week.

If you answered b:

Just because you're on probation doesn't mean the law doesn't apply. Most employment laws still cover you while on probation, including the right to be paid overtime.

If you answered c:

This is a pretty good option, because it costs you nothing, and you're legally protected from retaliation for doing it. You might want to try option a first, and if they don't pay, contact the Department of Labor.

Scenario 15

You're on probation. Your boss calls you into his office, puts his hand down your pants, and says, "Go ahead, report me. You're on probation. You don't have any rights." Do you:

- ❏ a. Punch him in the face, run, and scream for help?
- ❏ b. Report him to HR under the company's sexual harassment policy?
- ❏ c. Do and say nothing? You don't want to be fired.

If you answered a:

You're probably at risk of being arrested, and certainly of being fired. You can't be violent at work, even in self-defense.

If you answered b:

This is what the Supreme Court says you must do. You must report it and give them a chance to fix the situation. Being on probation does not affect your right to work free of sexual harassment.

If you answered c:

You'll probably be harassed over and over. He'll keep accelerating the attacks. At the very least, please start writing down dates, times, and any witnesses. You should report this, in writing, to HR as soon as possible.

The Basics While You're Working:

Wages, Hours, Breaks, Benefits, Sick Time, E-Mail, Social Networking, At-Will, Right to Work

The Company Says I'm Exempt From Overtime. Can That Be Right?

If your employer is treating you as exempt from overtime, odds are they got it wrong. Just because you're salaried doesn't mean you're automatically exempt. Most employees are entitled to be paid overtime (1.5 times your regular hourly rate) under the Fair Labor Standards Act (FLSA) for any hours worked over 40 per week. Some employees are exempt, but not nearly as many as most employers and employees assume.

Here are some ways you might be exempt from overtime.

Specific Jobs Excluded: This includes movie theater employees, live-in domestic employees, farm workers on small farms, railroad employees (you're covered by the Railway Labor Act) and truck drivers, loaders, helpers, and mechanics (covered under the Motor Carriers Act), computer professionals making at least $27.63/hour, commissioned sales employees who average at least 1.5 times minimum wage/hour, auto dealer salespeople, mechanics and parts-people, and seasonal and recreational workers. Here are some other employees who are exempt from all or part of FLSA:

Salaried Employees: If you make less than $23,600 ($455/week) you're never exempt. If your employer cuts your pay if you miss part of the workday, you're not exempt. But they can deduct from your leave bank or paid time off (PTO) if you miss work. You can't have your salary reduced if there is no work or if work is slow. You can be docked for missed full days due to disciplinary suspension, sick days, or personal leave. But even if you're salaried, you're still not exempt from overtime unless you also have exempt job duties.

Executive Duties: If you're salaried and they don't take improper deductions, then you're exempt if you supervise two or more employees, if management is your primary job, and if you have genuine input into the hiring, promotion, and firing of your subordinates.

Learned Professions: This exemption includes doctors, lawyers (not paralegals), dentists, teachers, architects, clergy, RNs (not LPNs), engineers, actuaries, scientists (not technicians), pharmacists, and other learned professions. (This usually requires an advanced degree.)

Creative Employees: Creative employees who are exempt include actors, musicians, composers, writers, cartoonists, and some journalists. People in this category don't necessarily have to be paid on a salary basis to be exempt, but they still must make at least $455/week.

Administrative Duties: If you perform office or nonmanual work that's directly related to management or the general business operations of your company or their customers, and you are regularly required to use your independent judgment and discretion about significant matters, then you might be exempt. An administrative assistant who is the CEO's right hand is probably exempt, but the secretary to a mid-level manager probably isn't.

Retaliation: The employer isn't allowed to retaliate against you for objecting to not being paid overtime or minimum wage. But that doesn't mean they won't do it. If you do object, make sure you're right, and put the objection in writing so that you have proof you objected before you were fired.

Consequences: For the employer who gets this wrong, the consequences are potentially huge, because the courts will allow your lawyer to bring in the other employees who also weren't paid correctly, and make the company pay them, too.

Donna's Tips >

- ⊃ If you're regularly working over 40 hours per week, check with the U.S. Department of Labor or a lawyer to see if you're owed money.

- ⊃ Unpaid overtime owed may also give you leverage to negotiate a better severance package if you're fired or laid off.

- ⊃ If you object to not being paid overtime when you aren't really exempt, you may be legally protected from retaliation.

The Company Says We Don't Get Any Breaks. I'm Entitled to Breaks, Right?

Almost everyone I talk to about this issue is absolutely sure they're entitled to two 15-minute work breaks and one lunch break a day. Almost everyone is wrong. Those very sure people frequently smart off to their bosses, who demand they get back to work. Those people are usually unemployed shortly thereafter.

Before you say you intend to finish your coffee, you should know that federal and most state laws do not require work breaks. Not for lunch. Not for rest. Not for coffee. Zero. Zip. Not for the bathroom. Can't hold it? You can be fired. Is this any way to treat employees? No. But employers can be big jerks and get away with it in many states.

However, if you need breaks as an accommodation due to a disability, then the employer may have to grant them.

Here's what the law does say about breaks.

Payment for Breaks: If the break is 20 minutes or less, the employer must pay for it. If it's over that, the employer can deduct for the time taken as a break. If the employer makes you work or permits you to work during your break, they must pay you for that time.

Non-Meal Breaks: Very few states require some non-meal breaks for adults.

Meal Breaks: Close to half the states have meal break requirements for adults, or at least some jobs held by adults.

Child/Teen Labor: The Fair Labor Standards Act (FLSA) restricts the number of hours people under the age of 16 can work. Some states have additional limits on child labor, and some have restrictions on employees over age 16. FLSA also restricts teens and children from working in certain dangerous occupations.

Breaks for Medical Conditions: Certain health conditions require work breaks. For instance, diabetics may need to eat periodically and may need an insulin shot during the day. Other conditions require breaks for medications, rest periods, and frequent bathroom breaks. If you need a work break regularly for health, speak to your healthcare provider about seeking an accommodation under the Americans with Disabilities Act or intermittent leave for partial days under the Family and Medical Leave Act.

Nursing Mothers: You do have a federal law that protects you. The FLSA, which applies to most employers, says that, if you aren't exempt from overtime, you're allowed reasonable unpaid breaks to express breast milk until your child reaches 1 year of age. However, employers with fewer than 50 employees are exempt from this if they show an undue hardship. Employers also must provide a place (other than a bathroom, shielded from view, and free from intrusion from coworkers and the public) for you to express. Many states provide more protections for nursing moms, and some cover smaller employers.

Bathroom Breaks: OSHA is the most likely agency to care if your employer won't give you bathroom breaks. There really is no law requiring them. OSHA requires bathrooms, but doesn't explicitly require bathroom breaks. They require that any physical restrictions on bathroom use, such as locking doors and making employees request a key, be "reasonable." However, denying reasonable bathroom breaks is probably a health hazard, so you might complain to OSHA if this is what is happening. Because there's no law requiring bathroom breaks, there's also no protection from retaliation if you complain about it to your boss. If you go to OSHA and complain, though, you're likely a protected whistle-blower, which means the employer can't retaliate.

Donna's Tips

⊃ Keep track of your work breaks. Punch in and out accurately if you have a time clock. Otherwise, keep accurate records of all your time.

⊃   If you work at your desk or if your employer calls you back to work mid-break, keep track.

⊃   Don't demand breaks you're not legally entitled to. If you are entitled to a break, then you probably can't be fired for objecting to having your break denied. However, if you get it wrong and insist on a break you're not entitled to, your company can fire you for insubordination.

⊃   Your union contract might require some breaks. If the employer isn't giving breaks you bargained for, contact your union rep.

⊃   If you need a work break for a medical condition, the time to seek an accommodation is before you are disciplined.

They Have to Provide Health Insurance, Don't They?

No federal law requires your employer to carry health insurance coverage for employees (a few states, including Massachusetts and Hawaii, are different). However, once they do have coverage, there are federal requirements employers must follow. If your employment has ended, read the paperwork you get regarding COBRA to find out your rights to continued coverage. If you're still employed or about to be employed, here's what you should know about your insurance.

Non-Discrimination: Your employer must not discriminate in providing or reducing coverage based on, for example, age, disability or pregnancy.

Plan Description: The Employee Retirement Income Security Act (ERISA) requires your employer to provide a description of your plan and how to make claims.

Privacy of Records: If your employer has access to medical records, such as when they're self-insured, they must comply with the privacy requirements of the Health Insurance Portability and Accountability Act (HIPAA).

Specific Coverage Requirements: Certain procedures must be covered once insurance is provided. For instance, if mastectomies are covered, then reconstructive surgery must also be covered. Insurance can't restrict the length of hospital stays for the birth of a child to less than 48 hours for vaginal delivery or 96 hours for C-section.

Preexisting Conditions: HIPAA limits exclusions for preexisting conditions to no more than 12 months, and allows plans to look back no more than six months. Pregnancy and genetic information (absent an actual diagnosis of the genetic condition) can never be excluded. If you were covered by a prior plan and had less than a 63-day break in coverage, preexisting conditions aren't excluded. Most children can't be excluded based on preexisting conditions. Right now, the prohibition on excluding you due to preexisting conditions applies to "grandfathered" group plans but not individual plans. The prohibition on excluding employees for any preexisting condition starts in 2014.

Health Factors: You can't be denied insurance or have benefits reduced due to your health status, physical or mental illness, claims experience, receipt of healthcare, medical history, genetic information, conditions arising from domestic violence, participation in hazardous activities, or disability.

Certificate of Coverage: The employer must provide a certificate of coverage automatically at certain times, and upon request.

Young Adults: Your plan must allow you to have your children covered up to age 26.

Lifetime Limits: No lifetime limits on coverage are allowed anymore. Most plans can't have annual limits.

Rescission: If you become ill, the insurance company can't look for unintentional mistakes on your application as an excuse to deny coverage.

Eliminate or Reduce Coverage: Your employer can eliminate coverage or change plans at will.

> *Donna's Tips*

- ⊃ Your employer must disclose if it believes its plan is "grandfathered" and exempt from some of the new healthcare reform's requirements. If it is grandfathered and significant changes are made to the plan, it might lose its grandfathered status and have new requirements.
- ⊃ Non-grandfathered plans must provide access to pediatricians and OB-GYNs, and coverage of preventive services with no cost sharing.
- ⊃ Read your plan and understand it. Don't wait until a crisis to understand your healthcare coverage and rights.

They've Accused Me of Excessive Absenteeism, but All I Did Was Use My Earned Sick Time. They Can't Fire Me for That, Can They?

Ninety percent of life is just showing up.
— Woody Allen

Woody was right. You must show up to work, even on Mondays. Most companies keep track of Monday absences in particular, since those are the most likely to be wine flu or sick-of-work-itis. Excessive absenteeism will get you fired more commonly than almost any other reason. Yet employees seem shocked when they get fired for missing work. *But I had a doctor's note! But I had a flat tire. But my car broke down.*

Your boss doesn't want to hear excuses. Your boss wants you at work.

That doesn't mean that there aren't any laws protecting you if you miss work for a legitimate reason. Here are some types of absences that might be protected.

Serious Medical Condition: If an immediate family member or you have a serious medical condition, you may be protected by the Family and Medical Leave Act (FMLA) if you've been there at least a year and if your employer has 50 or more employees. FMLA allows up to 12 work weeks in a 12-month period.

One way to qualify for a serious health condition is making two visits to a healthcare provider within 30 days of the first day you can't work or your family member is sick. (The first visit must be within seven days of the first day of incapacity.) Another is if you have more than three consecutive full calendar days of incapacity plus a regimen of continuing medical treatment. (The first doctor visit still must be within seven days of the first day of incapacity.) As for chronic serious health conditions, "periodic visits" are defined as at least two visits to a healthcare provider per year.

FMLA also allows intermittent leave or part-time employment until you've used up the equivalent of 12 workweeks in a 12-month period. Time spent doing "light duty" work doesn't count against your FMLA leave entitlement. Your right to get your job back is held in abeyance during the period of time you do light duty (or until the end of the applicable 12-month FMLA leave year). If you're voluntarily performing a light-duty assignment, you're not on FMLA leave.

Disability: If you miss work due to a disability or medical treatment needed for a disability, you might be protected under the Americans with

Disabilities Act (ADA) if your employer has at least 15 employees. The ADA may allow more leave than 12 weeks as long as it doesn't cause an undue hardship for your employer.

The ADA also allows part-time work or occasional time off as a reasonable accommodation if it doesn't impose an undue hardship on your employer, and if you can perform the essential functions of your job while working part-time. If reduced hours create an undue hardship, your employer must see if there is a vacant, equivalent position you're qualified for that you can be reassigned to without undue hardship while you're working a reduced schedule. If an equivalent position isn't available, your employer must look for a vacant position at a lower level for which you're qualified. Continued accommodation isn't required if a vacant position at a lower level is also unavailable. Your employer and you may also agree on other accommodations, such as a transfer.

Pregnancy: Title VII, which is the law covering discrimination, including pregnancy discrimination, requires that all leave policies in effect also apply to pregnancy if your employer has at least 15 employees. If longer leaves are given to employees for any reason, they must be given to pregnant employees. A seemingly neutral policy that prohibits any employee from taking sick leave or short-term disability leave during the first year of employment could possibly violate Title VII, even though it would be in compliance with FMLA.

Testimony Under Subpoena: In some states, your employer can't fire you for missing work due to being subpoenaed to testify, or for the content of your testimony. This means they can't fire you even if you testify against them.

Jury Duty: In most states, and for all federal courts, you can't be fired for missing work due to jury duty.

Military Service: You can't be fired for missing work due to military service. The Uniformed Services Employment and Reemployment Rights Act of 1994 (USERRA) requires reinstatement with seniority and doesn't depend on the employer's size.

Military Family Leave: FMLA provides caregiver leave for families of covered military members. Family members of covered service members can take up to 26 weeks of leave in a 12-month period. Covered family members are spouse, child, parent, or next of kin.

Sick of Work: Sorry, not covered.

Paid Leave: No federal or state law requires paid sick leave.

Donna's Tips

➲ Many states, counties, and municipalities have laws that offer additional protections. Some examples of absences that may be protected in your area are domestic violence, voting, medical leaves for smaller employers, and disability accommodations for smaller employers.

➲ Check your handbook. Your employee handbook will detail what procedures your employer expects you to follow if you're going to be absent. Follow their procedures to the letter.

➲ If you have a sick kid, don't lose your job! Check around to see if your area has any sick child daycares. They'll usually be a hospital or medical facility with nurses on duty to keep an eye out, follow doctors' instructions, and dispense medications.

➲ Unless you qualify for FMLA leave or have a disability for which you are seeking accommodations, your employer can fire you for any reason, including absenteeism. Know what they consider excessive. If you must come to work sick, that's better than losing your job.

➲ If you are contagious, then your employer requiring you to come in anyhow might be an OSHA violation. You can point this out, but don't be insubordinate.

➲ If ordered to come in, then rent a stretcher if you must. Unless going to work endangers your life, comply with the boss's order to come to work. Appeal to HR if you can, but don't lose your job.

Can I Sue If I'm Hurt at Work?

If you are injured at work, you probably can't sue your employer. Instead, you'll likely have to make a workers' compensation (workers' comp) claim. An employer that carries workers' comp insurance is mostly immune for suits for workplace injuries. Here's what you need to know about workers' compensation claims:

Intentional Injuries: Assault, battery, defamation, and other intentional torts are usually not covered by workers' comp.

Coworker Liability: Your coworkers are also likely immune from suit for workplace injuries if the employer has workers' comp insurance. However, they could be personally liable for assault, battery, defamation, and other intentional torts.

Making Claims: You must follow the employer's claim procedure for workers' comp claims. This usually means you must report the injury to your supervisor, who must prepare an injury report to file with the state workers' compensation board. You must notify your supervisor as soon as possible, providing the date of injury, witnesses, and how the injury happened.

Light Duty: If your company has light duty, they may have to provide it to you and you will get workers' comp benefits that make up the difference. But many employers will deny they have light duty, and you may lose coverage because you're able to work. It's important to speak with a workers' comp attorney before you try to go back to light duty.

Work-Related Injury: If the injury happens at work or is related to work, such as when you're running an errand for work, then it may be covered.

Retaliation: Generally, your employer can't retaliate against you for making a workers' comp claim.

Donna's Tips

⊃   Don't delay if you're injured. If you wait months before making the claim, your employer may not believe that you were injured at work. The sooner you make your claim, the better your witnesses' memories will be.

⊃   Workers' comp requirements are tough to navigate sometimes. If you have a serious injury, you probably need to talk to a workers' comp attorney.

Am I Entitled to Family and Medical Leave?

FMLA may apply if you have a serious health condition, which can be a broken arm, chicken pox, or other health condition that is temporary but causes you to be unable to work for at least three days or if you require any inpatient treatment. FMLA also applies to permanent conditions that require treatment, such as heart problems. FMLA covers care for family members. If you take FMLA leave, the employer must restore you to the same or an equivalent (pay, benefits, duties, hours, location) position when you return. Here's what you need to know about Family and Medical leave:

Employers Covered: All companies that have at least 50 employees. All public agencies. All public and private elementary and secondary schools.

Employees Covered: You must have worked 1,250 hours during the 12 months before the start of leave, work at a location where 50 or more employees work within 75 miles of, and have worked for the employer for 12 months. The 12 months doesn't have to be consecutive. If you were gone less than seven years, you can count your prior work with the employer. If your break in service was due to military service or covered by an agreement like a union agreement, then it can be longer than seven years ago.

Serious Health Condition: Illness, injury, impairment, or physical or mental condition involving inpatient care or continuing treatment by a healthcare provider. You may have a serious health condition if you make two visits to a healthcare provider within 30 days of the beginning of incapacity (the first visit must be within seven days of the first day of incapacity), if you have more than three consecutive full calendar days of incapacity plus a regimen of continuing treatment (the first visit must take place within seven days of the first day of incapacity), or if you've had any inpatient treatment (overnight stay) or need follow-up care for any inpatient treatment. For chronic, serious health conditions, "periodic visits" are defined as at least two visits to a healthcare provider per year.

Military Families: Family members of covered service members can take up to 26 weeks of leave in a 12-month period in certain circumstances. Covered family members are spouse, child, parent, or next of kin.

Definition of "Family Members Covered": Spouse, child, parent. Includes biological, adopted, or foster child, stepchild, legal ward, or a child for whom you stood in the shoes of a parent. Non-parents who acted as your parents may also be covered.

When You Can Be Fired While on FMLA Leave: You can still be fired/demoted/required to change jobs while on FMLA leave if there's a legitimate disciplinary action (for instance, you're arrested or do something wrong while on leave); there's a reduction in force; you were hired to complete a particular job or project and it ends; your leave exceeds 12 weeks; you fail to provide adequate notice; you fail to return to work; you're unable to perform all your job duties; your license expires; or you give notice of intent not to return.

Donna's Tips >

> ➲ The employer must post FMLA procedures. They also probably have the FMLA process in the handbook. There are lots of hoops to jump through, so make sure you comply.

> ➲ The company can make you give medical certification regarding your serious medical condition, but still must meet healthcare privacy requirements. If they must contact your doctor for additional information, it can only be to complete the certification form. They can't ask for medical records.

> ➲ You can be required to get a fitness for duty certification before you return to work. Make sure you find out what the employer needs well before your return date so you can return on time.

Can My Employer Monitor My Internet Usage?

Your employer can, and probably will, monitor your Internet usage at work. Assume that every single page you look at will be reviewed by someone in the company. You don't have any right to privacy for sites you view on your office computer.

Many employers prohibit personal use of their computers. So do your online shopping, buy your airline tickets, and check your Facebook and Twitter pages on your home computer. If you visit a pornography site, even accidentally by clicking a link in an e-mail when you don't know what it is, you can be fired. Here's what you need to know about computer use at work:

Social Networking: If you have a Facebook, MySpace, LinkedIn, Plaxo, Twitter, or other social networking account, assume your employer or potential employer will see what you've written. This is not the place to publicly air confidential information or grievances against your boss. It's also not the place to post racy photos.

Disabilities and Genetic Information: If the employer finds out about a disability or genetic information by looking at your social networking, they aren't allowed to use it against you for hiring, promotions, or discipline. Still, be careful what you publish.

Business Events: If you attend a business event, be careful what photos you post or allow others to post on-line. If you are photographed sitting on a coworker's lap drunk, you might be slapped with sexual harassment charges. Photos of you in a public place are probably fair game for the Internet. Conduct yourself accordingly.

Vacation and Activities: If you've called in sick, don't post your cruise pictures or photos of the party you had during your sick leave. Seriously.

Restrictions: If you claim you need light duty or accommodations for a disability, don't post photos of yourself doing heavy lifting or physical activities.

Donna's Tips

- ⊃ Think before you post. Assume your boss and potential employers will read every word and peruse every photo, and govern yourself accordingly.

- ⊃ Don't review anything, forward anything, or post anything from your work computer that isn't work-related. You're supposed to be working. Work while you're at work, and play on the computer at home.

Can My Employer Read My E-Mails at Work?

Assume your employer is monitoring your e-mails at work, and act accordingly. That means no forwarding of "funny" e-mails in bad taste; no writing your lawyer from your work e-mail address; no writing love notes to coworkers; no writing anything you don't want published in the company newsletter.

Time after time, I see people who, after whistle-blowing or reporting sexual harassment/discrimination, are suddenly accused of having porn on their computers. That's because clever employers know almost everyone has some inappropriate e-mails they failed to delete or, worse, forwarded. Those e-mails just may give your employer the so-called "legitimate reason" they need to defend against a retaliation claim.

This is an emerging area in employment law. Here are some (fairly lame) protections from e-mail snoopery:

Electronic Communications Privacy Act of 1986: This act prohibits interception of your e-mails, but has exceptions for consent (which applies if your company has a policy on e-mail interception or had you sign an agreement, a handbook, or anything else they managed to slip in front of you agreeing to this). It also has exceptions if the company is the e-mail provider or if they monitor your e-mail in the ordinary course of business, such as for customer service. Just assume this law probably doesn't help you, until the courts say otherwise.

Intrusion on Seclusion or Privacy: State tort claims might help in some cases. Some states offer protections for highly offensive conduct that's intrusive, assuming that you can prove you had an expectation of privacy. For example, you're your boss activates your computer camera to watch you change clothes in your locked office, you might have a claim for intrusion on your privacy. These cases are tough to win in most states.

Attorney-Client Privilege: At least to the extent you're checking your personal e-mail account from your work computer, some courts protect attorney-client communication. But don't assume you're safe. Assume someone is reading anything you do on your work computer. Even if they can't use it in court, knowledge is power.

Donna's Tips

- ⊃ Before you open an e-mail, be sure of the source. Even if you open something from a friend without knowing its contents, if it contains pornography or something inappropriate, you can be fired for having it.

- ⊃ Don't forward anything you wouldn't forward to your mother, your 7-year-old, and your spouse. If you wouldn't want them to read it, assume you'll get fired if the boss sees it.

- ⊃ Before you write anything, assume your boss will see it, and word it carefully.

- ⊃ Get out of the habit of using "reply all" and instead hit "reply." Carefully select the recipients of each e-mail.

Is it Okay for Me to Insult My Boss on Facebook?

You may have heard about the case the National Labor Relations Board (NLRB) brought against a company for disciplining an employee based on insults she posted on her Facebook page about her boss. As a result of the publicity this case got, lots of employees are posting nasty comments about their bosses on Facebook, tweeting about how awful management is, and then wondering why the heck they were fired.

Please, please don't post anything in any form of social media you don't want on the front page of the company newsletter. Don't get fired over something stupid. Here's what you need to know before you criticize your boss:

Concerted Activity: The "concerted activity" provision of the National Labor Relations Act (NLRA) applies whether or not the company has a union, and covers pretty much every workplace. HR people and management-side lawyers don't like to talk about it because it covers anything employees do for mutual aid or protection. Here's what it says: "Employees shall have the right to self-organization, to form, join, or assist labor organizations, to bargain collectively through representatives of their own choosing, and to engage in other concerted activities for the purpose of collective bargaining or other mutual aid or protection."

If you're complaining about working conditions—not just your own but also those of your coworkers—you're possibly protected from retaliation under NLRA. Does that mean you should rush to post what a jerk your boss is? No. Not unless you want to be fired.

Over-Broad Policies: NLRB says policies prohibiting all disparaging comments when discussing the company, supervisors, or coworkers are illegal. Similarly, policies that prohibit employees from depicting the company in any way in social media may also violate the NLRA. However, companies may (and probably should) have social media policies that define what employees will be disciplined for when they use social media.

Coworker Input: If you're just venting without encouraging coworkers to weigh in, you might not be protected. If, for instance, you never friend coworkers on Facebook, then you rant about work, you aren't engaging in "concerted activity" that's protected. If you post, thinking it will generate a discussion, and it doesn't, you may or may not be protected. So tweeting that your boss is a jerk when your coworkers don't follow you or comment is probably not protected.

Protesting Working Conditions: Cases where employee comments were protected include an employee who was fired for criticizing unpaid, two-hour sales meetings (also probably protected under the Fair Labor Standards Act and some other whistle-blower laws, by the way); employees who were terminated for sending a letter protesting working conditions and saying that they were being told to spend large amounts of time on the company president's pet project; and an employee who got a written warning for objecting to a supervisor's lecture about radio headset volume. So yes, protesting poor working conditions may well be protected under NLRA.

Intention Is Key: Your intent is all-important. If your employer thinks your intent was to retaliate, damage your boss's reputation, damage the company, or anything but to improve working conditions, then you're probably going to be unemployed.

No Solo Act: Your comments must be part of "concerted activity," which is defined as "being engaged in with, or on the authority of, other employees, and not solely by and on behalf of the employee himself." If you go it alone, you do it at your peril.

False Accusation: If you are fired for suspicion of being involved in discussions with coworkers or activity protesting or objecting to workplace conditions, you are still protected even if you weren't actually involved.

When You Might Not Be Protected: There are also lots of exclusions, so many employees aren't protected. Since the NLRA is meant mostly to protect attempts to unionize, supervisors, independent contractors (yeah, yeah, most employers get this wrong), domestic workers, agricultural workers, family member employees, and managerial and confidential employees aren't protected. If you're high enough up, you can't gripe and get away with it.

The Company Policy Might Be Okay: The NLRB has found other provisions in employer policies didn't violate the act. For instance, language prohibiting "disparagement of company's or competitors' products, services, executive leadership, employees, strategy, and business prospects" was allowed.

Procedure for Violations: If you think you were fired or disciplined for criticizing your boss, and you're pretty sure you are protected, don't sit on your rights. You only have six months to file a complaint with the NLRB. They will investigate to determine whether or not there's cause for your charge. They may interview you, at work if you're still there. You can have a union rep or coworker present. A report then goes to the regional director, who decides whether or not the case will go forward. Mostly, the cases are dismissed. Only about one-third of all cases go forward. If you're dismissed, you can appeal to the general counsel's office.

If the regional director finds reasonable cause, then they'll first try to settle it. About 90 percent of the cases settle at this stage. If it doesn't settle, it goes before an administrative law judge, and NLRB staff counsel will represent you. You can also have a private lawyer with you, but the lawyer's role is limited, because the case is not yours, but the NLRB's.

If you win, you can get reinstatement, back pay, and interest. You cannot get emotional distress. The statute doesn't provide for an award of attorney's fees, but sometimes they can be awarded as a "sanction." The judge can also order the employer to cease and desist their illegal practices.

Donna's Tips

- ⊃ I still suggest you shut your mouth about any complaints you have, especially in social media. There are just too many ways you can mess yourself up, and the law has too many loopholes to give you much aid and comfort.

- ⊃ Let's not forget there's still not a single state that has passed a law against workplace bullying. The bottom line is that a bully boss still has the power to discipline you, decide whether you get raises or promotions, and make your life miserable. Why tick him or her off if you aren't protected from retaliation?

- ⊃ The First Amendment doesn't protect you unless you work for the government (or unless somehow your company works with government to restrict your free speech, which is unlikely to apply to your situation). There's no free speech in corporate America.

- ⊃ Because you may not be able to recover attorney's fees, it may cost you more than you end up winning if you hire an attorney to represent you. Most people who go through this process are represented by their union. If you aren't unionized, you might have to represent yourself if you can't afford a lawyer.

- ⊃ Protest to your elected representatives if you don't like the law. If enough voters complain, things will change.

What Does it Mean When My Employer Says I'm an At-Will Employee?

Most states are at-will states, meaning an employee can be fired for any reason or no reason at all. No good reason is required. Only one state (Montana) requires employers terminate only for just cause. Although there is a Model Employment Termination Act that legislatures can easily adopt if they want to assure employees can only be terminated justly, no state has passed it.

The concept of at-will employment is a shock to most people, who believe that their employer must have a reason in most states. The truth is that the employer can walk into the office in a bad mood and fire people with few consequences. The employer doesn't even have to give a reason. The only way to change that is to urge your state legislators or Congress to pass more protections for employees.

That doesn't mean there are no protections for employees. You should ask yourself the following questions to see if you might be covered under some employment law:

Did My Supervisors Make Any Comments Indicating Bias? If your supervisor made racist or sexist jokes, said she thought you were too old or your disability made you unable to do the job, required you to work on religious holidays, or made other comments that would indicate a bias, you may have direct evidence of discrimination.

Was I Treated Differently Than Others in the Same Situation? If you don't have direct evidence of discrimination, you may be able to demonstrate you were treated differently than those of a different race, sex, religion, national origin, age, or other protected status under the same circumstances. Try to think of people who are of a different race, age, sex, and so forth, who were treated differently from you. Find out if there are people who have also been the victims of similar discrimination.

Why Was I Really Fired? Most employees have a pretty good idea why they were fired. If you made a workers' compensation claim and were fired a week later, that's a good indication you were fired in retaliation for making the claim. If you reported your supervisor for Medicare fraud, and then the supervisor fired you, you may have a whistle-blower claim.

Am I in Some Protected Category? If you were fired after you took protected action, you may be able to sue for retaliation. Think about whether you recently made a workers' compensation claim, performed jury duty, served in the military, took family/medical leave, served as a witness in a lawsuit, provided testimony or evidence to the EEOC, refused to participate in illegal activity, reported illegal activity, complained about working conditions along with coworkers, or engaged in protected free speech.

Exceptions: Most states have some exceptions to the at-will doctrine, such as prohibiting retaliation for making workers' compensation claims, objecting to illegal activities or discrimination, testifying under subpoena, and serving on jury duty. Some states don't recognize any of the three major exceptions, but have some statutes that accomplish some of the same things. The exceptions are:

Public policy exception. This is where the termination violates an established state public policy, such as refusing to participate in illegal activity or termination for making a workers' compensation claim. Several states don't recognize this exception.

Implied contract exception. This is most commonly applied to employee handbooks and requires employers to follow their own policies. Most states follow this exception, though several don't.

Covenant of good faith exception. This exception reads a covenant of good faith and fair dealing into all employment relationships, and means either that employer personnel decisions are subject to a "just cause" standard, or that terminations made in bad faith or motivated by malice are prohibited. A few states allow this exception.

Donna's Tips ▷

⊃ Even if nothing illegal happened, many employers will discuss a severance agreement. Sometimes an amicable transition is the best way for both employer and employee to move on in a positive direction. If you are offered a severance package, it you may want to have an attorney review it prior to signing. Many employment attorneys will work to negotiate a better package for you.

⊃ Many people (including lawyers) will say, quite knowingly, that their state is a "right to work state," as if this means the employer can terminate for no reason. This makes no sense, for a good reason: Those people are using the wrong terminology. "Right to work" means the employer cannot require the employee to join a union in order to work for them.

My Employer Says the Employment Laws Don't Apply to Them. Can They Be Right?

They might be, but then, most employers are covered by some employment laws. Every employment law defines which employers are covered under it differently. Companies in the United States, U.S. companies employing U.S. citizens in foreign countries, and foreign companies controlled by U.S. companies generally must comply with U.S. laws. Employment agencies and labor organizations are usually covered as well. Here's what yu need to know about which laws cover your employer:

Title VII (discrimination) and Americans with Disabilities Act: Applies to employers with 15 or more employees during 20 weeks of the last year. Does not apply to private membership clubs that are tax-exempt, most aides to elected officials, some religious organizations, Native American tribes, and some organizations involved in national security.

Age Discrimination in Employment Act: Applies to employers with 20 or more employees during 20 weeks of the past year. Applies to all state and local governments.

Family and Medical Leave Act: Applies to employers with 50 or more employees within 75 miles of your work location. All public entities and private elementary and secondary schools are covered. Unions with 25 or more members are covered.

Fair Labor Standards Act: Applies to employers with $500,000 in gross yearly sales; that have employees engaged in interstate or foreign commerce; that have employees producing goods for interstate or foreign commerce; or that have employees handling, selling, or working on goods that have been moved in or produced for interstate or foreign commerce. In other words, almost every company. Does not apply to churches and charities.

National Labor Relations Act: Covers all private employers whose activities affect interstate commerce (in other words, most private employers). They have specific requirements for the amount of revenue particular types of employers must generate to be covered. Government entities, Federal Reserve banks, wholly owned government corporations, religious organizations with religious purposes, employers that employ only agricultural laborers, and employers subject to the Railway Labor Act are not covered.

Donna's Tips

⊃ If you think your employer isn't covered, make sure you're counting independent contractors who might really be employees. Also check any affiliated companies. Sometimes they might be considered a joint employer or integrated enterprise whose employees must be counted together. When in doubt, contact the agency that handles the type of violation (such as the EEOC, Department of Labor, or OSHA) or an attorney in your state.

⊃ Cruise ships operating in international waters still must comply with discrimination laws, but otherwise admiralty law applies to them (a whole, weird area of law involving everything from shipboard injuries to treasure hunting).

⊃ State laws and city/county ordinances may well cover smaller employers, so don't give up until you've checked with your state and local agencies or a lawyer in your locality.

The Company Says I'm Not an Employee

Many people believe their employers when they're told they're not employees, so they think employment laws don't apply to them. Don't fall into this trap.

If you perform services for someone and they control what you do and how you do it, you're probably an employee. Some employers will try to classify you as an independent contractor to get out of paying their portion of employment taxes and to keep from counting you for purposes of discrimination and other employment laws. It's best to assume you're an employee for most purposes until your lawyer or the IRS tells you otherwise, and to not rely on your employer to decide your status.

It makes a difference who is an employee and who isn't. If you're an employee, your employer is subject to the Fair Labor Standards Act and may have to pay overtime for weeks worked over 40 hours. Most employment laws state a minimum number of employees the employer must have before the law applies to them.

If you think your employer is too small to be covered by discrimination laws, Family and Medical Leave, whistle-blower, or other laws, make a list of everyone who works there, part-time or full-time, even people labeled "contractors." Those contractors are probably employees, too.

Owners don't count as employees for purposes of most employment laws. But sometimes partners or "owners" are that in name only. If you are a shareholder or partner in a business but are still subject to firing and discipline, you may well be an employee covered under employment laws.

Volunteers or interns who do work for the company that replaces the work of an employee, or who do extra work even without being told, are still likely employees who must be paid. While there is a "volunteer" exception, it's not applicable to most employers. Many intern programs are run poorly and result in the intern being an employee. If you offer to work for free at a company, they probably won't say yes because they must pay at least minimum wage and overtime.

Donna's Tips

➲ Don't sign away your rights as an employee. Some employers will try to get you to sign an independent contractor agreement. Have a lawyer review it before you sign if you are in doubt about your rights.

➲ Even if you think you've signed away your rights, have a lawyer review your job duties and who controls your work before you give up. Wage/hour/overtime laws can't usually be waived by contract.

➲ The IRS has some tests it uses to determine whether you are an independent contractor. There's a handy-dandy form called the SS-8 you can fill out to have the IRS find out if you're really a contractor. If an employer isn't paying in their portion of your employment taxes and you think you're an employee, you can report them to the IRS.

Is My Unpaid Internship Legal?

You've been offered a great opportunity: an internship with a company in your dream industry. The only problem? They won't pay you. These opportunities can be the foot in the door you need, but they can also be an excuse to exploit a young person unaware of their rights. Here are some questions to ask yourself to determine whether your unpaid internship is illegal:

Training: Are you being given training similar to that you would receive in a vocational school? In other words, are you learning something you can use in your future career? Or are you stuffing envelopes and filing? The internship must give you training. Your tasks should build on each other so you develop more skills, similar to the way each chapter of a textbook builds on the others.

Benefit: Is the training for your benefit? Who is getting more benefits—the company or you? It should be you.

Supervision: Are you being closely supervised? You shouldn't be working on your own or displace a regular employee.

Advantage: Does the employer receive an immediate advantage from your work? If they can make money off what you're doing, or if you're saving them from having to pay another employee, you probably must be paid.

Guarantee: Are you guaranteed a job at the end of your training period? If so, you're probably a trainee that needs to be paid.

Understanding: Was it made clear that you wouldn't be paid at the time you were hired, or was this something that was sprung on you after you started? If you didn't understand that you weren't entitled to wages for the time you were training, you're probably entitled to be paid.

Consequences: Many employers get internships wrong. The consequences to the employer are harsh. They could have to pay your wages, overtime, liquidated damages equaling the wages they failed to pay, and your attorney's fees.

The most important thing to do before accepting an internship is get a clear understanding of your job duties, whether you'll be paid, and what the employer expects. If it doesn't sound like you'll get a great learning experience, then turn it down unless you absolutely need it for your resume or as a job requirement. It's your time, and time is money. Make sure you get your money's worth out of your internship.

The U.S. Department of Labor (DOL) is not amused when employers get this wrong. They are cracking down on unpaid internships that are really jobs.

Donna's Tips

➲ If your internship isn't what you thought it would be, and the opportunities promised don't pan out, you can come after them two years (sometimes three) for the unpaid wages. That means you can wait to see if you get that job offer before you sue.

➲ If your employer is getting this wrong, you can sue on your own behalf and on behalf of all the other interns who didn't get paid. That means some wage and hour lawyer is rubbing his hands together with glee when you contact him. It also means you might have more leverage than you think to negotiate payment.

➲ If you're asked to sign a contract waiving your right to be paid, contact an employment lawyer in your state to review it. It may be unenforceable, but why take chances? Be sure before you sign.

➲ When in doubt, contact the DOL to see if they can help you figure out if you should be paid.

I Work for a Native American Tribe and They Say the Employment Laws Don't Apply to Them

If you work on a reservation for a Native American tribe, U.S., state, county, and local laws do not protect you. Native American tribes are sovereign nations and cannot be sued under most U.S. laws. That's a surprise to most people working for tribes in casinos, restaurants, and shops throughout the United States. Here's what you need to know about working for Native American tribes:

Contracts: Tribes can waive sovereign immunity through certain contracts. If you're negotiating an employment contract, that's the time to ask that you be allowed to sue if they violate anti-discrimination and other laws—but don't hold your breath: It's more likely that the tribe you're working for signed an agreement with the U.S. government or a large corporation waiving immunity. If you're working on a project that's federally funded or in which a U.S. corporation is involved, there may be a waiver.

Some Statutes That Might Apply: Some courts have held that certain federal laws apply to businesses owned by tribes. The National Labor Relations Board will hear claims of violations of NLRA regarding businesses owned by Native American tribes. Courts have held both ways on the applicability of several federal statutes to tribally owned businesses. Depending where you live, the NLRA, FLSA, FMLA, OSH Act (Occupational Safety and Health Act), and ERISA might apply to tribal businesses.

Tribal Courts: You can appeal your termination and raise issues such as discrimination to the tribal courts for your employer's tribe. Each tribe has different procedures. It's unlikely you'll get much relief there, but it's worth a shot.

Donna's Tips

⊃   Working for a Native American tribe is risky. You're likely not covered by workers' comp, unemployment, or other laws that protect employees. Know what you're getting into before you go to work.

⊃   The upside is that many tribes have loads of cash to spend on lucrative jobs. If you take a tribal job, sock away as much money as you can, while you can.

Who Owns My Social Media Contacts and Posts?

Most employees think their social media is none of their employer's business. So who owns your social media contacts and posts? When you leave, it is possible for your former employer to make a claim to some or all of your social media contacts or posts. Here's why:

Contracts: Remember that pile of stuff your employer handed you when you first started? They said to sign it and you were anxious to start working and not make waves, so you signed without reading. They might not have even given you a copy. Maybe they handed you an agreement after you were working for a while that you signed. Well, you must read that stuff and understand what you're signing next time. If you think you signed any agreements, ask for a copy, and make sure you know your rights and responsibilities. Here are some examples:

Non-compete agreements. Most states allow employers to say you can't work for a competitor for a year or two after you leave, as long as they have a legitimate interest to protect, such as trade secrets or confidential information. That means that if you leave and start friending all your former customers on Facebook, linking with competitors, and posting that you're looking for work in the same field, you'll probably get a letter from the company lawyer asking you to stop.

Non-solicitation agreements. Even if you're allowed to work for a competitor, you might have agreed not to solicit employees, customers, and/or vendors of the former employer. Some employers demand that former employees unlink and de-friend their LinkedIn, Facebook, and other social network contacts connected with the company. An employee who leaves and starts sending connection requests to their old client list, corporate buddies, and vendors can be in a world of hurt if the company thinks they're violating their non-solicitation agreement. Many courts that won't enforce non-competes will still enforce a non-solicitation provision, so be careful. However, the fact that information is available on social networks such as LinkedIn may be evidence that it is not a trade secret.

Intellectual property agreements. If you signed an agreement saying anything you create while you work for the employer belongs to the company, then your employer might own your blog, Twitter account, or other social media you do on work time, especially if you're blogging or tweeting about the company. Some agreements have clauses saying if you thought about it or created it during the term of your employment, even on your own time, your employer owns it. If you think they don't own your novel, toy designs, or video game programming, you may be wrong.

Confidentiality agreements. Many companies have employees sign agreements saying they will keep confidential company information a secret. If you blog, write a novel, or tweet about the inner workings of the company, you might be accused of violating your confidentiality agreement. Also, some employers have non-compete and non-solicitation provisions in documents called "Confidentiality Agreement." Most people don't read what they sign. Failing to read is no excuse. You're likely bound by what you sign.

Work for Hire: If you were hired to be the company blogger, tweet for the company, or develop the corporate media presence, the work you did while you were employed and those social media accounts you got for the company likely belong to the employer.

Trade Secrets: If you are the safekeeper of the KFC secret recipe, know the formula for Coca Cola, or have access to anything that would be of value to a competitor and that the company keeps secret (client lists, manuals, or pricing—anything kept from the public) you can't blog or tweet about it without getting in trouble. Even if you didn't sign an agreement, most trade secrets are protected by state and federal law. On the other hand, if it's on the company Website or available publicly, it's not a trade secret.

Donna's Tips

⊃ People are sometimes surprised when I tell them to talk to their former employer about this stuff. Most businesses don't want to be in litigation any more than you do, and may work out reasonable restrictions and accommodations. Don't hide what you're doing or sneak around. A judge or jury might see this as evidence of a guilty conscience.

⊃ If you aren't sure whether the company will let you keep your blog, mind if you connect with customers after you leave, or care if you work for a competitor, ask them in writing (via e-mail, fax, or something that provides proof they got it). Tell them what you're doing and why you think it doesn't violate your agreement. Tell them you don't think it's a violation, but wanted to check. Give them a specific amount of time to object, such as 72 hours or five business days. Say that, unless they object by that time, you'll assume what you're doing is okay. If they don't respond, even if they claim later you breached your agreement, you then have proof that you asked. It may be evidence that they didn't act in good faith or waived their right to complain.

- ⊃ While most people continue to "own" their social media after they leave their employment, be very careful what you sign
  while you're employed. If you don't understand what you're
  signing, get an employment lawyer in your state to review it.
- ⊃ If you're being asked to sign a severance agreement, understand what you're signing. You might be agreeing to give up
  more than the severance is worth.

Is it Possible I Have More Than One Employer?

Even if your employer is too small to be covered by some employment
laws, it is possible you have another employer that, combined with your
too-small employer, has enough employees to be covered. Here are some
situations in which you might have more than one employer:

Integrated Enterprise: You may have more than one employer if your
company is owned and operated by someone or a group of people who
own other companies. The company is an integrated enterprise if the management, operations, and ownership are so interrelated that they are really a single employer. If, for instance, multiple companies have the same
HR department, one entity controls the other, managers work for more
than one company, or the ownership overlaps, you might work for an integrated enterprise. If only one entity makes the final decisions regarding
your employment, then you may not work for an integrated enterprise. In
at least one federal circuit, the integrated enterprise test no longer exists
for discrimination cases.

Joint Employer: If both entities share control over you, then they
might be your joint employer even if there is no common ownership.

Staffing or Temporary Employment Agencies: If your company out-
sources you, and your paycheck, handbook, and other personnel issues are
handled by a staffing agency, both the staffing agency and the company
might be your employer.

Donna's Tips

- ⊃ If your employer is too small to be covered, look at your
  paycheck. Is it issued by the company that calls itself your
  employer? If not, you might have more than one employer.

⊃ If you do work for multiple entities, keep track. If two or more companies give you assignments or supervise you, you might have more than one employer.

⊃ Is your human resources handled by another company? If so, that company may well be a second employer you can count.

I'm Only Five or 10 Minutes Late Every Day. Can I Get Fired for That?

Really? You're late every day, once a week, or even every month? How hard is it to get up 30 minutes earlier and haul yourself to work? You may think five or 10 minutes shouldn't make a difference, but it does.

Your supervisor has to deal with more than just you. If they allow you to come in five minutes late, then your coworker Suzy Snooze is going to whine that she shouldn't be held accountable if she's only 15 minutes late. Then Barry Barfly will say that an hour late is no big deal. It has to stop somewhere. They can stop it by firing you.

There are some possible protections you have for lateness, but they are very limited:

Family and Medical Leave: Assuming you have worked long enough and your employer is big enough, if you have doctor's appointments you need on a regular basis, then apply for intermittent FMLA. That way, if you must come in an hour late once a week or once a month, they can't hold it against you.

Disability. If your lateness is due to a disability or chronic medical condition, then you might be able to ask for a reasonable accommodation of occasionally coming in later.

Subpoena: If you were subpoenaed to testify at a trial or deposition, your state law possibly protects you from being terminated for your lateness.

Donna's Tips

⊃ If you are going to be late, let your supervisor know well in advance. Make sure you comply with the employer's reporting requirements. If you must let a specific person know, don't tell a coworker and assume she'll take care of it. You must personally speak to or e-mail or text the person you have to notify under your employer's reporting requirements.

⊃   It's best to confirm your notification in writing. Some unscrupulous supervisors will deny you called.

⊃   If your car breaks down, take a cab or get a ride. It's way
    cheaper than getting fired.

I Need Five Months off to Recover From My Illness. Can I Take a Leave of Absence?

Mostly, the law doesn't protect your right to return to work if you
take a leave of absence of more than 12 weeks. Here are some things to
consider when taking a long leave:

Employer Policies: Some companies have provisions in their policies
for longer leaves. Check your handbook and, if you think you qualify, contact HR.

Disability Insurance: If your company provides for short-term disability and long-term disability insurance and you're covered, you must
contact the insurance company and make sure you jump through all of
their hoops. If you are covered, you might be entitled to at least partial pay
during a covered absence.

Disability: If you are covered under the Americans With Disabilities
Act (ADA), longer leave might be a reasonable accommodation. If you
request a longer leave, mention ADA and make sure you get doctor's certification of the need for the accommodation.

Job Restoration: Once you've gone over your 12 weeks of FMLA
leave, you no longer have a guarantee that you'll be restored to your same
position. However, if there is an available position you qualify for when
you are able to return, the employer can't deny it to you just because you
had a medical condition.

Donna's Tips

⊃   If you have a medical condition that will require leave longer
    than what is covered by FMLA, scour your handbook and insurance policies for your options.

⊃   While on leave, keep checking in. Find out if your job will be
    there when you return. If they assure you that it will, confirm
    in writing.

⊃ A few weeks before your return date, check in again with HR. Make sure you get any doctor's certifications and other requirements taken care of. Confirm that your job will be open.

⊃ If you are replaced, find out what other jobs are available that you qualify for. They can't turn you down if you apply for a position you qualify for just because you had a medical leave. However, if someone better qualified applies, they don't have to give you preference.

Am I Entitled to Overtime for Working Holidays?

Lots of people think they're entitled to double time or overtime for working holidays. No federal law requires any additional pay for holidays over and above your regular pay rate for private employees.

If you work your regular 40 hours/week, you don't get extra pay for the holiday. However, if you work over 40 hours that week, you still get time and a half if you are not exempt from overtime. Here's what you need to know about holiday pay:

Union Contract: Some union contracts require extra pay for holidays. Whether time and a half or double time, holiday pay is something unions frequently negotiate, so check your collective bargaining agreement.

Employment Agreement: Extra pay for holidays is something you can negotiate in your employment agreement. If this is important to you, and if you have an employment agreement, the time to negotiate is before you sign.

Government Contractors: Some government contracts require employers to pay extra holiday pay.

Federal Employees: Federal employees may be eligible for premium pay on holidays.

Donna's Tips

⊃ Don't demand extra pay for holidays. If you refuse to work without extra pay, you can be fired for insubordination.

⊃ If you need a religious accommodation for a holiday, request it in advance.

⊃ If there's an emergency need for you to work on a holiday, suck it up. If everyone else is working, your absence will be duly noted and held against you.

Can My Employer Take Away the Company Pension Plan?

It's a long-term employee's worst nightmare: You've worked toward retirement and the company announces they're ending the company pension plan. Can they do this? Yes, they can. But you do have rights if the company decides to terminate most pension plans.

ERISA, the Employee Retirement Income Security Act, covers most non-government and non-church pension plans. In truth, most companies don't have what most people think of as pension plans anymore. What you probably think of as a pension plan is a defined benefit plan, promising a set monthly payment on retirement.

Most have switched over to a defined contribution plan, such as 401(k) plan or 403(b) plan, in which you have an account that the employer contributes a percentage of your income to, and you get the money that's in the account when you retire.

With either type of plan, the employer can terminate it, but there are rules:

Vesting: Once the plan terminates, you become 100-percent vested.

Defined Benefit Plans: These plans are generally insured by the Pension Benefit Guaranty Corporation (PBGC). If the employer is not in financial distress and wants to terminate, it either must buy an annuity that will pay out benefits as promised, or sometimes can pay a lump sum to beneficiaries.

Distress Termination: If the employer proves to a bankruptcy court or to PBGC that it cannot continue operations without terminating a defined benefit pension plan, then PBGC takes it over as trustee, pays benefits up to legal limits out of plan funds, and guarantees payments.

PBGC Termination: PBGC can terminate a defined benefit pension plan if it deems termination to be in the best interest of the participants.

Notice: If the employer is terminating the plan, the administrator must issue a Notice of Intent to Terminate giving 60 days notice. If PBGC terminates the plan, it issues a notice and then sometimes will publish the notice. After that, for a standard termination, you'll get notice within six months after termination describing the benefits you'll receive. If it's a distress termination or a PBGC termination, the second notice will be from PBGC once they've had a chance to review the plan records.

Donna's Tips

⊃ There is no insurance for a defined contribution plan such as a 401(k). That's because they are supposed to be fully funded all the time. However, if you are only partially vested when you leave, you will lose the unvested portion of your employer's contributions. If the plan terminates, the employer's contributions become 100-percent vested.

⊃ Enron highlighted a big problem with 401(k) and other defined contribution plans: having too much invested in your employer's stock. Diversify! If you have company stock that you are awarded periodically, sell part of it off on a regular basis. Eggs, basket. Capiche?

⊃ If you get a notice that your pension plan is terminating, read it carefully and understand what is happening. You may have to make some choices or take action to decide how you want to be paid. You also must start planning your future differently.

This Is a Right to Work State. So My Non-Compete Agreement Isn't Enforceable, Is It?

Lots of people think "right to work" means you have the right to work wherever you want. That would make sense, but since when has the law ever made sense? Right to work is where you can't be forced to pay union dues in order to work in a unionized shop. It has nothing to do with non-compete agreements. Zero. Nada. Zip.

Most states will enforce non-compete agreements to some extent. If you have one, check out the section on how to get out of your non-compete on page 226.

This Workplace Is Completely Unsafe. Can They Fire Me for Complaining?

The Occupational Safety and Health Administration (OSHA) is the government agency that regulates safe working conditions. You are legally protected from retaliation for complaining to OSHA, seeking an OSHA inspection, participating in an OSHA inspection, and participating or testifying in any proceeding related to an OSHA inspection.

Depending on your industry and what type of safety violation you complained about, you have some hoops to jump through and deadlines to comply with if you want to take legal action against your employer for retaliation:

By Telephone or in Writing: If you are being retaliated against for complaining under these laws, you can complain to OSHA about the retaliation by telephone or in writing (I recommend writing): Occupational Safety and Health Act (30 days); Surface Transportation Assistance Act (180 days); Asbestos Hazard Emergency Response Act (90 days); International Safe Container Act (60 days); Federal Rail Safety Act (180 days); National Transit Systems Security Act (180 days).

In Writing Only: If you are retaliated against under these laws, your complaint to OSHA about the retaliation must be in writing: Clean Air Act (30 days); Comprehensive Environmental Response, Compensation and Liability Act (30 days); Energy Reorganization Act (180 days); Federal Water Pollution Control Act (30 days); Pipeline Safety Improvement Act (180 days); Safe Drinking Water Act (30 days); Sarbanes-Oxley Act (180 days); Solid Waste Disposal Act (30 days); Toxic Substances Control Act (30 days); Wendell H. Ford Aviation Investment and Reform Act for the 21st Century (90 days).

Types of Retaliation: Examples of types of retaliation you are protected against include denying benefits, failing to hire or rehire, intimidation, reassignment affecting promotion prospects, reducing pay or hours, firing or laying off, blacklisting, demoting, denying overtime or promotion, and disciplining.

Refusal to Work: You have few protections from retaliation if you refuse to perform a job duty due to hazardous conditions. You are protected only if you believe that you face death or serious injury and the situation is so clearly hazardous that any reasonable person would believe the same thing; you have tried to get your employer to correct the condition; there is no other way to do the job safely; and the situation is so urgent that you do not have time to eliminate the hazard through by calling OSHA or other government agencies. If you walk off the job, you are not protected at all.

State Agencies: If your state has an OSHA-approved safety plan, you may also need to file with your state agency. Whereas OSHA only covers private employers, state plans frequently cover government entities as well. You may also have additional state whistle-blower protections for reporting safety violations. In some states, you might also be able to claim wrongful discharge in violation of public policy.

Disruption: Your employer can fire you if you argue, become disruptive, or otherwise violate company rules. Make sure you object calmly.

Donna's Tips

- ⊃ OSHA proceedings are tough to win, so be careful when you complain. Make sure you are objecting to something so unsafe that it's worth losing your job over.

- ⊃ Don't walk off the job. If you refuse to perform a job duty because it will kill or maim you, stay on the jobsite. If you are sent home, make sure you confirm with HR that you are being sent home and that you aren't walking off the job.

- ⊃ If OSHA decides you don't have a claim, you can't file a lawsuit on your own. But you might still have protection under state laws, state tort law, or another federal law because the laws are so complex. You might want to get an attorney if you think you are being retaliated against for objecting to a safety violation.

- ⊃ Most claims are under the 30-day deadline. If you remember to complain in writing within 30 days from the date of retaliation, it's hard to go wrong. (Note that, unlike most laws, you don't get until Monday if your deadline is Saturday, Sunday, or a holiday.)

The Company Says They Are Cutting My Rate of Pay, Retroactive to Last Month. Can They Do That?

Your employer must pay you for all the time you worked, at the rate they agreed to pay you. A retroactive pay cut is not legal under the Fair Labor Standards Act and most state laws. That means if, for instance, your employer says your hourly rate just went from $12 to $10, they can't say it went into effect last week or even yesterday. If your annual rate went from $50,000 to $40,000, the reduction must start after they announce the decrease.

An employer can further never reduce your wages below minimum wage, whether retroactively or in the future.

If you have a contract setting out your pay rate, it probably also says the contract can only be modified in writing signed by both parties. That means you can enforce your pay rate. On the other hand, if the contract also says you can be fired at will, they can probably fire you for declining a pay cut. If you refuse a pay cut, you will probably qualify for unemployment when you're fired for refusing it. However, if you work with the pay cut for a while and then quit, you may not qualify, because you will be deemed to have accepted the pay cut.

Donna's Tips

- ⊃ Think carefully if you're told you are getting a pay cut. It might be better to take the cut and start looking elsewhere than to lose your job altogether.

- ⊃ If you decline the pay cut, put it in writing that you respectfully decline it. Let the company fire you rather than quit so you will have the right to collect unemployment.

- ⊃ If the company says that, if you continue to work, you will be deemed to accept the cut, you might have to resign. Put it in writing along with the reason for the resignation and that you were forced to resign.

The Company Stopped Paying My Wages or Is Bouncing Checks. What Are My Rights?

In this economy, more and more employers are simply not paying employees. Either they do it the slow way, by getting further and further behind and begging for patience, they bounce checks, or they simply don't pay. I've had too many people come and see me only after the employer is tens of thousands of dollars in the hole and the employee is in a financial bind.

If your employer is starting to pay late, bounce checks, or not pay at all, find another job as soon as you can. Work is not your hobby. Don't do it for free.

Here are some claims you may have against your employer for late or non-payment:

Bounced Checks: This is likely a crime in your state. You may also have some civil remedies that include penalties like double or triple damages.

Wage Theft: More and more states and local governments are passing laws saying it's a crime to not pay employees within a certain amount of time. If you aren't paid, one thing you can do is call the police department for help.

Fair Labor Standards Act: The Department of Labor handles complaints of non-payment of wages. You can call them if you aren't paid.

Minimum Wage: Federal law provides for a minimum wage. Many states have minimum wage laws that require higher pay (but never lower) than the federal law. If you aren't paid anything for a particular time period of working, you obviously weren't paid minimum wage. Minimum wage laws carry penalties, and government agencies are more willing to get involved with this type of violation than other wage disputes.

Breach of Contract: If you have a contract providing your pay rate, then the company may be in breach.

Bankruptcy: If the company files for bankruptcy, you must file a claim as a creditor in the bankruptcy court. You should be a priority claim as an unpaid employee, but you might need help from a bankruptcy attorney.

Donna's Tips

⊃ If the employer stops paying, bounces a check, or only pays part of what is owed, consider that a warning sign. Get the heck out of there as soon as you can.

⊃ If you're working for free, think about the time you could be spending with your family or on real hobbies instead. I don't care how much they beg, or how good their intentions are, few employers manage to dig themselves out of a financial hole that keeps them from paying employees.

⊃ If you forego pay, your supervisors, company owners, and other higher-ups should certainly do so as well. Your pay shouldn't be used for the owner's Tahiti vacation.

⊃   If you forego all or part of your pay, ask the company to sign a promissory note. They'd make you sign one if you asked for a loan. That's what you're doing: giving them a loan.

Crisis Scenarios for Your Basic Work Questions

Scenario 1

You're dog tired. You've been working for four hours and you can't think straight anymore. You tell the boss, "I'd like to take my break now." She says, "No. I'm not allowing breaks today. We're too busy." Do you:

❑ a. Say, "I know my rights. I'm entitled to my break," then stomp off to the break room?

❑ b. Mutter under your breath and complain to coworkers about your boss being a jerk? Make it clear to her by slamming things, snippy responses, and bad attitude that you are unhappy.

❑ c. Say, "Okay. I'm really tired though. Can you let me know if there's a good time later?"

If you answered a:

You're probably getting written up or fired for insubordination. No federal law requires any work breaks for meals or rest. Only a few states require any non-meal breaks for adults. Even if you're in one of the lucky few, you still can't safely disobey a direct order from the boss without getting into trouble.

If you answered b:

Expect a write-up for having a bad attitude. If you were snippy or irritating enough to your boss, you might get fired. You've demonstrated you are unprofessional and immature. Don't count on being promoted anytime soon.

If you answered c:

You've demonstrated that you are concerned about your boss's needs. You are putting the company ahead of yourself. Because you answered reasonably, your boss might start looking for a less-busy time to give you a break. Even if it stays busy, you probably went up a notch or two in her estimation.

Scenario 2

Same as scenario 1, except you need to use the restroom. You know you can't hold it much longer. Do you:

❑ a. Say, "Gotta pee! Can't hold it anymore," and hop off to the rest room holding yourself?

❑ b. Walk over to the nearest potted plant, unzip, and let nature take its course?

❑ c. Get close to the boss and whisper, "Sorry, but I really need to use the restroom. I promise I'll be quick."?

❑ d. Pick up the phone and call human resources, then report her to OSHA?

If you answered a:

Maybe you skate because the boss doesn't want to clean up a puddle. But you have abandoned your post, been insubordinate, and showed you have zero class. The chance you are written up or fired is 50/50.

If you answered b:

You may as well pack up your stuff and leave. There is only one circumstance where this might be an option. If the boss says you will be fired if you go to the bathroom (and this does happen), then the potted plant scenario is an option only if you can do it very quietly and not be seen by your boss, coworkers, or customers. This is a last-ditch possibility for only the worst, most bullying bosses.

If you answered c:

You probably get the okay to go, since your boss doesn't need the mess. You've shown you understand the problem by promising not to waste time. Maybe she asks you if you can wait a few minutes before you go. If you can, then do. If you can't, tell her it's an emergency. You probably should have spoken up before you got to that point, so your boss knows you aren't planning ahead. But it beats the heck out of having an accident.

If you answered d:

You've walked off the job, so you're being insubordinate. This is only an option if you had to resort to the potted-plant scenario. If your boss is a bully and enjoys making employees suffer, you probably should report her. If it's a first-time situation, then HR is the place to go. If the boss or the company has a no-breaks policy even for restroom breaks, then they may be violating workplace safety laws. You should report them to OSHA.

Scenario 3

You get a salary and your supervisor says you're exempt from overtime. You always must work through lunch and stay at least an hour late. You supervise one person and do mostly clerical work. Your boss requires you to get approval for everything you do. Should you:

❑ a. Sue the bastards? You know you're entitled to overtime.

❑ b. Not say anything? You're probably exempt from overtime.

❑ c. Keep track of your real hours and report them? If you aren't paid for overtime, keep a record of how much you are owed. Wait a few months, then take the time records to the Department of Labor or a lawyer that handles the Fair Labor Standards Act to find out if you're really exempt.

If you answered a:

You're probably right, but you risk being wrong. The laws on exempt employees are pretty tricky, so you might want to contact an expert first and get an opinion. If you don't keep good track of your hours, you'll have to estimate, which is much harder to prove than if you write it all down.

If you answered b:

You're probably losing out on overtime pay that you're entitled to. Under these facts, you probably are not exempt.

If you answered c:

This is the smart move. If you're right, then you'll be able to make an informed decision as to whether to go to HR first with the problem, file a complaint with the Department of Labor, or sue. You'll have good records and you will have kept your options open.

Scenario 4

Same as scenario 3 except that you supervise two people, and your clerical work is filling out bid paperwork relating to the key jobs your company works on. You have discretion as to how to fill out the forms, and your boss pretty much rubber stamps what you prepare. Do you:

❑ a. Sue the bastards? You know you're entitled to overtime.

❑ b. Not say anything? You're probably exempt from overtime.

❑ c. Keep track of your real hours and report them? If you aren't paid for overtime, keep a record of how much you are owed. Wait a few months, then take the time records to the Department of Labor or a lawyer that handles the Fair Labor Standards Act to find out if you're really exempt.

If you answered a:

You're probably wrong. You may well be exempt. You might have to pay the company's court costs, and possibly even their attorney's fees, if you lose. You're now on their permanent you-know-what list.

If you answered b:

You're probably right. You should still keep track of your real hours and never report fake hours (every day 8.0, for instance) just in case it turns out you are not exempt.

If you answered c:

You're not wrong to do this. If you aren't exempt, you still have your options open

Scenario 5

After you start working, you ask about how to get on the company health insurance plan. They say they don't have one. Do you:

❑ a. Demand coverage? Throw a big fit if they don't comply. Threaten to sue.

❑ b. Make sure you pay your COBRA premiums from your last job and start looking for private coverage?

❑ c. Report them to the state's insurance department? They're breaking the law.

If you answered a:

You're fired. Or at least written up for insubordination. They don't have to provide insurance unless you live in one of the few states that require it. If you do live in one of the lucky states, contact the state agency that handles insurance issues and find out the process for complaining. Then complain quietly.

If you answered b:

Smart move. Because they don't have to provide coverage, you'd better make sure your family and you are covered.

If you answered c:

Good luck with that—unless, that is, you're in one of the few states that require health insurance, and then this might be exactly where you must file a complaint.

Scenario 6

Same as scenario 5, except they say that, while they do have coverage, they don't cover people with preexisting conditions. They ask if you have any preexisting conditions, and you disclose that you're diabetic. They refuse to submit your application and send out a memo warning everyone not to give you candy because of your condition. Do you:

❑ a. File a complaint with EEOC? They are engaging in disability discrimination.

❑ b. Contact an attorney about the company's violation of your HIPAA privacy rights?

❑ c. Contact an attorney about the company's violation of ERISA?

Ha! Trick question. All of the choices are right. This HR person is a big screw-up. They'll end up making some attorneys on both sides of the fence some money.

Scenario 7

You have a nasty cold and you call in sick. Your supervisor reminds you that you have a big project due tomorrow and asks you to finish it. Do you:

❑ a. Say, "Hey, I'm sick. Get someone else to do it. I know my rights. You can't make me work when I'm sick."?

❑ b. Smack yourself in the head because you're so sick you forgot? Drag yourself into work and finish the project. You can collapse after you finish and turn it in.

❏ c. Put in for Family and Medical Leave, and ask for an accommodation under the Americans With Disabilities Act to be allowed to turn it in late?

If you answered a:

You probably won't have a job when you come back. There's no legal right to sick leave. That will teach you to put off a big project to the last minute.

If you answered b:

You've kept your job. Good thinking. Try to stay away from coworkers so you don't spread the illness.

If you answered c:

Sorry. A cold is not protected under FMLA or ADA. Your request will be denied and the project will still be due. Better get cracking.

Scenario 8

Same as scenario 7, except the illness is that you have had a heart attack and are being rushed to the hospital when you call. Do you:

❏ a. Say, "Hey, I'm in the hospital. Get someone else to do it. I know my rights. You can't make me work when I'm in the hospital."?

❏ b. Smack yourself in the head; you're so sick you forgot? Show up on a gurney if you must. At least you won't lose your job.

❏ c. Ask for Family and Medical Leave, and ask for an accommodation under the Americans With Disabilities Act to be allowed to turn it in late or to get someone else to finish it? Fill out the paperwork as soon as you are able.

If you answered a:

You're probably right, but the attitude won't be appreciated. If you leave them in the lurch, you will not be in anyone's good graces. Though the person demanding that you come in isn't being very sensitive, he's probably stressed if it's a big project.

If you answered b:

For heaven's sake. No job is worth dying over. Get to the hospital.

If you answered c:

> You've covered yourself (or had a family member cover you) legally. Do what you can to tell them where everything is and recommend someone who can finish it. Now, get yourself better.

Scenario 9

You've had a bad year with your health. Nothing serious, thank goodness. Two days with a cold. You stubbed your toe and had to go to the urgent care a week after you got back and missed a day. Then you had a car wreck and missed a day to get checked out. You had an allergic reaction to shellfish and missed two days the following month. You get a warning: any more absences and you'll be fired. You haven't exhausted your sick leave yet. You get a terrible headache a month later and can barely think straight. Do you:

□ a. Call in sick? You are entitled to use your sick leave.

□ b. Go in? Take a taxi if you can't drive. You can't afford to lose your job.

□ c. Go to the doctor and get a note? They can't fire you if you have a note.

If you answered a:

> You're probably fired. They don't want to hear excuses. You were warned. There's no legal entitlement to sick leave.

If you answered b:

> Congratulations. You saved your job. Now do your best to get your work done. Take an aspirin. Go to the urgent care after work if you still feel sick and get it taken care of.

If you answered c:

> You're probably still fired. Just because you have a note doesn't mean you have any legal protection.

Scenario 10

Same as scenario 9, except the headache is due to chronic debilitating migraines. You've been getting medical treatment for years for this horrid condition. The doctor says you must be out for three days so she can adjust your medication. Do you:

❑ a. Call in and tell them what's happening? Get a note. Tell them when you will be back in and show up when you're cleared.

❑ b. Ignore the doctor and go in, on a gurney if you have to? You can't afford to lose your job.

❑ c. Call when you get back from the doctor and know how long you will be out?

If you answered a:

This is the right move if you've worked at least 1,250 hours in the past 12 months, you have worked at least a year, and the company has 50 or more employees within 75 miles of where you work. You're likely covered by FMLA. You're possibly covered by ADA if they have at least 15 employees, but migraines may not be a covered disability.

If you answered b:

This is the right move if you haven't been there 12 months, you work part-time, or if the company is too small for FMLA coverage.

If you answered c:

You might be fired, even if you're covered by FMLA. Unless you are incapacitated and unable to call, you should call in as soon as you know you will be missing work.

Scenario 11

You're at work when a large box falls from a high shelf and hits you in the head. You have a knot on the back of your head but feel okay. Do you:

❑ a. Tell human resources and ask them to fill out a report of your injury, to make sure you're covered by workers' compensation?

❑ b. Call an ambulance? Don't bother telling anyone what happened until you get a diagnosis.

❑ c. Call a personal injury lawyer? You can sue and retire.

If you answered a:

Good job. You will be covered by workers' comp if it turns out you're seriously injured. If the employer wants you to go to their workers' comp doctor, do it.

If you answered b:

Dumb move. You can't just disappear in the middle of the day. If you are seriously injured and feel like you must go to the hospital, by all means call 911. But then let your supervisor know what's going on or make sure a coworker goes to get some help.

If you answered c:

You've been watching too many late-night commercials. If your company is covered by workers' comp, you can't sue; you must file a workers' comp claim. Fortunately, the personal injury attorney's office will probably tell you that.

Scenario 12

Same as scenario 11, except HR tells you that they don't carry workers' comp. The next day, you're laid off for lack of work. Do you:

❑ a. Contact the agency in your state that handles workers' compensation? Report the company for failing to have insurance. Then go to your own doctor.

❑ b. Contact a workers' compensation attorney? He or she might be able to file for you even if the company isn't covered.

❑ c. Contact a personal injury attorney? If the employer doesn't have coverage, they aren't immune from suit.

❑ d. Contact an employment attorney? You might have a claim for wrongful termination for making a workers' compensation claim.

If you answered a:

You're right.

If you answered b:

This is also right.

If you answered c:

Probably right again. However, if the injury isn't serious, a personal injury attorney probably won't touch it.

If you answered d:

Correct, too.

Any of these moves is a good first step. You may have multiple claims against this employer. Explore your options before making a decision.

Scenario 13

You're on Family and Medical Leave. You're scheduled to return to work in two days. You get a FedEx package that says your position has been eliminated. You find out the person who was hired to work temporarily to fill your position has been hired permanently, but the title of the position has been changed. Do you:

❑ a. Contact the Department of Labor or a lawyer? They've broken the law.

❑ b. Sigh and apply for unemployment? You're allowed to lay people off even if they're on leave.

❑ c. Apply for another available position in the company that you're qualified for?

If you answered a:

If you've been replaced, then you're right. The law requires that they restore you to the same or an equivalent position. A one-person layoff that is a sham, even with a title change, probably doesn't cut it.

If you answered b:

You should apply for unemployment, but if you don't pursue your legal claims you might be missing out on some remedies you're entitled to.

If you answered c:

Good move, too, especially if you have filed a FMLA claim. If they are having a real restructuring, they might be able to fit you in. If they deny you a position that's available, it might be considered retaliation.

Scenario 14

You're called into HR and presented with a stack of printouts from your computer. IT has been monitoring your internet usage. They've found travel Websites, job search Websites, and, worst of all, porn. You're asked to sign a final warning for violating the Internet usage policy. Do you:

❑ a. Sign it and consider yourself lucky you weren't fired?

❑ b. Ask to see the times of the Web searches? Compare it to the times you were working. If you weren't there, maybe it was the cleaning crew or a coworker.

❑ c. Contact a lawyer? Your privacy has been violated.

If you answered a:

Dude. You were caught. You're right to sign it. Now make sure you only do work on your computer. Play at home. Don't open strange e-mails or attachments/links from friends who send funny but inappropriate jokes. Tread very carefully. You are very lucky to still have a job.

If you answered b:

If you're sure none of these are yours, go for it. However, if you clicked some links or opened pictures that were inappropriate, even if you closed them immediately, you're still responsible. Be more careful next time.

If you answered c:

Odds are the employer had the right to monitor your Internet usage. However, in some states you might have more rights, so it could be worth asking.

Scenario 15

Same as scenario 14, except they used keylogging software, which logged your passwords. They then went into your Facebook account using your password and read the messages your coworkers sent you complaining about your supervisor. You were fired. Do you:

❑ a. Sign the termination papers? You were caught red-handed.

❑ b. Contact a lawyer about this invasion of your privacy?

❑ c. File a complaint with the National Labor Relations Board?

If you answered a:

Number one, what possible reason would you have for signing any paperwork once you've been fired? Unless they're offering some severance or something else if you do sign, you shouldn't sign anything they shove in front of you when you're already gone. You're too upset to think. Second, you do have potential claims against them here. They didn't have the right to access your passwords or private messages.

If you answered b:

Hopefully the lawyer will look into some possible privacy claims. There are some keylogging cases that are making their way through the courts, especially where passwords and private messages were accessed.

If you answered c:

You'll probably succeed. If you were fired for engaging in concerted activity with coworkers to address working conditions then the employer violated the National Labor Relations Act when they fired you for it.

Scenario 16

You write to an employment lawyer complaining about national origin discrimination at work using your personal e-mail, but on your work computer. HR calls you in the next day and fires you, waving the e-mail in your face. Do you:

❑ a. Let the lawyer know right away? The employer has violated attorney-client privilege.

❑ b. Contact the police? They have intercepted your communications illegally.

❑ c. File a retaliation complaint with the EEOC?

If you answered a:

You should definitely let the lawyer know that the communication wasn't confidential. There may be legal consequences for a potential case down the line. Whether or not you waived attorney-client privilege may depend on what state you live in. Never communicate with your lawyer on a work computer/device or using your work e-mail.

If you answered b:

You're probably out of luck. Odds are the employer had the right to monitor any e-mails you sent on your work computer or using your work e-mail. However, some states do have legal protections, so it might be worth a try.

If you answered c:

If you are fired for complaining about discrimination, normally you are protected from retaliation. However, it's up in the air whether you can be fired for talking to an attorney about bringing a discrimination claim. I would say yes, but some courts disagree.

Scenario 17

Your boss tells you that you'll get the promotion only if you sleep with him. You say no, of course. The person who gets the promotion clearly didn't turn him down. There's no sexual harassment policy and no HR department. There are only 10 employees. Do you:

❑ a. Start looking for another job? Avoid being alone with this jerk.

❑ b. File a charge of discrimination with the EEOC? That's sexual harassment.

❑ c. Check your state and local laws and ordinances to see if they protect employees of smaller companies from sexual harassment?

If you answered a:

That's probably your best bet. The employer is not covered by any federal laws against sexual harassment.

If you answered b:

They'll turn you away. The employer is too small to be covered by the EEOC or the federal laws they administer. You might want to re-count employees for the company. If you're excluding independent contractors, employees of other companies this guy owns, or related companies, you might be counting wrong.

If you answered c:

Good idea. Some states, counties, and municipalities have laws covering smaller employers. If your locality doesn't, maybe it's time to talk to your representatives about passing something so others don't have to go through what you just went through.

Scenario 18

Same as scenario 17, except the employer has 20 employees and you are an independent contractor. Do you:

❑ a. File with EEOC?

❑ b. Cancel your contract and move on?

❑ c. File an SS-8 form with IRs to see if you're really a contractor?

If you answered a:

This is probably a good move. Odds are, you're misclassified. Unless you're absolutely sure you are properly classified as a contractor, don't let him get away with this awful behavior. He'll do it again.

If you answered b:

If you're truly a contractor, this might be your only option. However, if you're doing work for a government contract the employer has, you might still have some remedies, so see if you can get your hands on the contract they have with the government. It should be public record. Some state and federal laws apply to people who work for government contractors.

If you answered c:

While the IRS's determination that you're an employee might carry some weight with a judge, a jury, or the EEOC, it's not binding. Still, it would have some influence on the matter, and the employer might be more encouraged to settle if IRS has said they're wrong. You'd still have to file with the EEOC on time, so don't miss your deadline waiting on IRS.

Scenario 19

You get your paycheck along with a notice that says, "Attention all employees: Due to financial problems, your pay is hereby cut by 25% until further notice, effective this paycheck." You look inside and, sure enough, it's 25-percent light. Do you:

- ❑ a. Send a notice to HR that you decline the pay cut and ask for your correct wages?
- ❑ b. Contact the U.S. Department of Labor to get the wages you are owed?
- ❑ c. Quit, then sue the bastards?

If you answered a:

This is a good move, especially if you don't have another job lined up. The result will likely be that you're fired, but at least you'll get unemployment. If you aren't fired, they're on notice that you don't accept the pay cut and, once you do find something else, you might be able to collect the difference.

If you answered b:

This may be your best option because you're now protected from retaliation. Hopefully they'll go after the company for the retroactive cut. If they do, they'll probably pursue it on behalf of your coworkers, too. If the DOL won't take it up, you might want to contact a lawyer who handles cases under the Fair Labor Standards Act.

If you answered c:

Never, ever quit without having another job lined up (unless your safety or health is at stake). You may not qualify for unemployment and it could be months before you find something else. You may, however, succeed in suing for the 25 percent cut on that one check. The better move would be to decline the cut and get fired.

Scenario 20

Same as scenario 19, except the announcement is that the pay cut will apply to your next paycheck. Do you:

- ❑ a. Contact the Department of Labor?
- ❑ b. Start looking for another job?
- ❑ c. Take a hard look at your employment contract to see what your rights are about your wages?

If you answered a:

You're probably out of luck. Unless you have a contract, the employer can cut your pay going forward with little or no notice.

If you answered b:

Good move. The company is in trouble. Time to bail, but do it after you get something else and on your own terms. The 25-percent cut will be hard, but not as hard as a 100-percent pay cut.

If you answered c:

If you have a contract, it might say it can only be modified in writing signed by both parties. If that's the case, then you might have a case for breach of contract.

Bad Stuff Happens:

Discipline, Bullies, Coworkers, and Harassment

I Disagree With My Discipline. Can I Refuse to Sign It?

Lots of employees refuse to sign disciplinary notices. Whether it's a counseling, warning, written reprimand, or suspension, anything before you're terminated is something you should sign. Why? Because refusing an order to sign it might be considered insubordination. It also makes you look like a.) a jerk; b.) unprofessional; or c.) you don't know what you are doing. Refusing to sign doesn't make it go away. They'll probably write on it: "Refused to sign." That looks good come promotion time, doesn't it? Here's what you need to know about your disciplinary notice:

But I Disagree With What it Says!: Okay, so what? Unless the document says your signature certifies you agree with it, you're merely signing that you received it. But I'm a cautious sort, so I recommend, just to be sure, signing, "As to receipt only; written rebuttal to follow." If it does say you certify that you agree with it, then write, "I disagree with this document and am signing as to receipt only." Get a copy. Always get a copy of everything you sign.

What Do I Put in the Rebuttal?: Be factual. This is not the time to insult your boss, complain about professionalism, or air general grievances. Be specific about what is untrue in the document. If you have proof, attach it. If you have witnesses, list them (but remember: Most coworkers will lie to save their jobs, no matter how much you think they're your friends).

Protected Categories: If you're working on your rebuttal, think about whether you were treated differently from others of a different race, age, sex, religion, color, national origin, or genetic information; who weren't disabled or pregnant; or who hadn't recently taken Family and Medical Leave, made a workers' comp claim, or objected to illegal activity. In other words, were you singled out due to some legally protected status? If so, now is the time to point that out.

But I Don't Want to Go There: Why the heck not? First of all, the Supreme Court says if you're being harassed or are in a hostile environment due to a protected status, you must complain under the company's harassment policy. Don't look at me like that. It's not my rule; it's the Supreme Court's rule. I know it's not practical. It's scary to go there. The Supremes say you must if you want to preserve your right to bring those claims down the road.

Second, if you complain about discrimination, whistle-blower retaliation, FMLA retaliation, workers' comp retaliation, or something legally protected, then you're also legally protected from retaliation. You not only should attach your discrimination complaint to your disciplinary notice, but you should also send it to HR or whoever is listed in the harassment policy.

You Didn't List Termination Papers as Something I Should Sign: Ah, I'm tricky that way. You're already gone. Why should you cooperate with anything the now-former employer wants you to do? I recommend against signing termination papers unless one of the following situations exists:

❯ The employer offers a severance package. Then you sign the termination form "as to receipt only," get a copy of the form, get a copy of the proposed severance package (which you should not sign yet), and take them to a lawyer to review.

❯ The employer is offering positive references and/or says they won't challenge your unemployment. Again, sign the form "as to receipt only," and get a copy of the form.

Always get a copy of the termination papers, whether or not you sign. If they won't give them to you, don't argue. I'm not sure what the point of not giving them would be, so maybe some of my HR readers can enlighten me.

Donna's Tips

➲ Most employers don't have to give you anything in writing about your termination. A few states do require they provide notice of termination so you can apply for unemployment, but most don't. Many employers won't even give a reason for the termination. That's because they don't have to. In some cases, the WARN Act (Worker Adjustment and Retraining Notification Act) may require notice of a mass layoff or plant closing though.

➲ If your employer asks you to participate in an exit interview, think about declining. Why put yourself through that? In most cases, don't bother. They don't care what a disgruntled ex-employee has to say. If you have a discrimination situation, put it in writing if you want to complain. Anything you say in an interview, and some things you never said, can and will come back to bite you later. If you complain verbally about discrimination, many HR people will deny it later. I've seen people who were accused of making threats or engaging in inappropriate behavior in exit interviews. Why be alone with Darth Vader? Just so they can see you cry or get angry? Fuhgeddaboudit.

➲ If you're making a discrimination complaint, call it a "Formal Complaint of [Racial, Gender-based, Religious, etc.] Harassment" and detail how you were singled out. List everyone of a different status who did the same thing who wasn't disciplined, or who wasn't disciplined as severely. List any comments your supervisors made about your protected status. Give them a chance to investigate. Don't expect much, but this will help you down the road if you ever decide to take legal action.

I'm Being Bullied and Harassed. Can I Sue?

Many employees have the mistaken belief that, if they are being harassed by a supervisor or coworker, they are in a "hostile work environment" and automatically have a claim against the employer. This is simply not the case. Although general harassment and bullying are legal in all states, some states have pending legislation on workplace bullying. Since 2003, many states have introduced workplace bullying laws, none of which have passed. Here's what you need to know if you're being harassed:

Illegal Harassment: The only harassment or hostile environment that is illegal is harassment due to race, age, sex, religion, national origin, color, disability, pregnancy, genetic information, objecting to illegal activity, taking Family and Medical Leave, making a workers' compensation claim, or engaging in activity that is otherwise protected by a statute (in some states, domestic violence leave, having a firearm in your vehicle, marital status, making a workers' compensation claim, sexual orientation, or because of testimony under subpoena). If your boss is just a jerk or abusive, that is not illegal. Many small employers are not covered by these laws, so you may not be protected at all.

Report It: A frequent mistake is this: "I was harassed, so I quit and then I told them why." The U.S. Supreme Court says that, where an employer has a published sexual harassment/discriminatory harassment policy, the employee must report it under that policy and give the employer the opportunity to fix the situation. If you did not report it under the employer's policy before quitting, you may lose your right to sue.

Employer's Duty: Appropriate remedies may be to discipline or warn the harasser, to move the harasser, under some circumstances to move the victim, to do training, or, in extreme cases, to terminate the harasser. But they don't have to take any action at all. They only have a duty to maintain a safe workplace. You might still have to work with the harasser.

What to Put in the Report: General harassment, hostile environment, bullying, and other disruptive behavior that is not due to a protected status or activity are not illegal. Before you write the long letter airing all your grievances against your boss, you may want to have an attorney look at it, or make sure you are addressing your protected status. If you do complain, put it in writing and call it "Formal Complaint of Sexual Harassment," "Formal Complaint of Religious Harassment," or whatever category you fit into. Set out the harassment due to your protected status, and be businesslike. This is not the time to air all your complaints about the business or your boss—only the specific complaint about the illegal behavior.

Donna's Tips

- ⊃ Many employees simply refuse to go back to work, even where the employer has warned or disciplined the harasser. Sometimes, the fear is justified. But it is the employer's duty to create a safe workplace. If you return and are retaliated against or continue to be harassed, report it again. If the employer allows retaliation or continued harassment, that is the time to get an attorney involved.

- ⊃ Employers will usually take accusations of this type of conduct seriously. Once they are on notice, they are liable if they allow it to continue, and they know it. Most employers know that this behavior is disruptive, has nothing to do with making money, and can adversely affect morale. Even if the employer takes no action, by reporting their inaction to the EEOC or your state agency, you have put these agencies on notice that this behavior is occurring. The employer will have no excuse when the harasser does it to the next employee. In some cases, you may have a remedy.

- ⊃ Whereas a long letter stating that your supervisor is incompetent or a jerk can and should get you fired, the formal complaint addressing illegal behavior should get a serious response.

- ⊃ Although bullying isn't illegal, harassment due to race, age, sex, national origin, disability, color, and religion is illegal.

- ⊃ If the bully is targeting certain age, sex, ethnic or other groups, they've probably crossed over into illegal harassment.

- ⊃ Bullies are a huge drain on corporate time and assets. Employers should adopt zero-tolerance policies regarding bullies. But even if they do, reporting bullies won't protect you from retaliation unless your state legislature or Congress wises up and passes an anti-bullying law.

Should I Complain About My Annoying Coworker?

You know how your parents hated when you argued with your sibling. Remember how they used to shout, "Shut up! I don't want to hear this petty bickering!'"? Well, your boss doesn't want to hear it either. The difference is, your parents had to put up with you. Your boss can fire you if you irritate them too much.

Coworkers are annoying, no doubt. Some will get up your nose worse than others. Mostly you should suck it up and take it. Do not write long tomes to your boss about how your coworker doesn't do his job, steals lunches, and plays music too loud. Your boss wants you to get along and get your work done. You should figure out how to do that.

It's not HR's job to act as referee for petty disputes between coworkers, either. They must deal with the serious stuff that's really illegal, not someone tapping their pen too loud.

Here's what you should report, and how you're protected if you decide to report it:

Discrimination: If you observe discrimination based on age, sex, race, national origin, color, religion, disability, genetic information, or another legally protected status, report it. If you report illegal discrimination, Title VII and possibly your state law protect you from retaliation.

Illegal Harassment: If you are the victim of or observe a coworker harassing someone due to age, sex, race, national origin, color, religion, disability, genetic information, taking Family and Medical Leave, reporting unpaid wages or overtime, making a workers' comp claim, whistle-blowing, or another protected status, then you should report it under your employer's harassment policy. You are protected under Title VII if you report discriminatory harassment. If you report harassment due to another legally protected status, then the law creating the protected status is the law protecting you from retaliation. For instance, FMLA, FLSA, local workers' comp laws, and most whistle-blower statutes have anti-retaliation provisions.

Reporting That's Not Protected: If you report a coworker for violating company policy, ethical violations, illegal activity that's not on behalf of the company, or bullying, there is likely no law that protects you from retaliation. Be very careful if you feel the need to report something that isn't protected. I've seen companies fire employees for reporting coworkers who were stealing from the company, with the reason being they should have reported it earlier. It's a no-win for the reporting employee. Depending on your corporate culture, rocking the boat may be dangerous to your continued employment.

Concerted Activity: If you are reporting a coworker who is making working conditions intolerable, and you are acting with coworkers, you may be protected under the National Labor Relations Act.

Donna's Tips

➲ Report it in writing. HR is there to protect the company. If they must testify, they'll frequently deny you reported anything legally protected and claim you reported general harassment or bullying.

➲ Focus your written complaint only on the protected status. For instance, if you're reporting sex discrimination, state all the sexist comments; the ways women are being treated differently; and the promotions, demotions, and firings that are gender-based. Avoid commenting about lack of ethics, bullying, and hostile environment that aren't hostile due to gender.

➲ Even if you can't live with your coworkers, you can't kill them. If you're even thinking about going postal, get some counseling. Talk to a spiritual advisor. Quit. Get the heck out of there. The jerk isn't worth life in prison. Sure, some people could drive you to the brink of violence, but any type of workplace violence will get you fired and probably get you tossed in jail. I know it can seem bad when you're in the middle of it—even desperate. But quitting is always an option. No job is worth your sanity, your safety, or your freedom.

My Supervisor Is Mocking Me Due to My Military Service. Can I Sue for Harassment?

There was a court ruling awhile back that harassing people at work for their military service was not illegal. Airline pilots sued, after being mocked and ridiculed at work due to their military service, for hostile work environment under the Uniformed Services Employment and Reemployment Rights Act (USERRA). USERRA says employers can't deny any "benefit of employment" due to military service. "Benefit of employment" includes "advantage, profit, privilege, gain, status, account, or interest." The court said USERRA "does not refer to harassment, hostility, insults, derision, derogatory comments, or any similar words. Thus, the express language of the statute does not provide for a hostile work environment claim."

Lucky for service members and former service members, President Obama signed the Veterans Opportunity to Work (VOW) to Hire Heroes Act of 2011. Along with lots of employer incentives and benefits for service people, this new law fixed the stupid loophole allowing harassment.

Donna's Tips

⊃   If you think you're being harassed due to your military service, report it in writing to HR and give them an opportunity to fix the situation.

⊃   If the company doesn't fix the situation and the harassment continues, or you are retaliated against for reporting the harassment, you have a legal remedy now under USERRA.

⊃   Don't harass people due to their military service. I don't care if you're anti-war. Number one, you'll be fired, and number two, have some respect for people who served their country.

I Reported Harassment and Now HR Wants to Meet With Me. What Do I Do?

I know it seems scary to report sexual, racial, or other harassment to human resources. It's even scarier when they call and say they've set up a meeting with their lawyer and you. It's tempting to refuse or delay this meeting. But being called into this meeting is actually a good sign. It means your employer is doing what they're supposed to do. (Either that or you're being set up to be fired, but let's stay optimistic.)

The Supreme Court says you must report discriminatory harassment under the company's published harassment policy and give them a chance to fix the situation. No excuses accepted, no exceptions made. (In Supreme Court-land, nobody is ever justifiably afraid of being beaten to a pulp, fired, demoted, or made miserable if they complain. Yeah, yeah, I know. But it's not my rule. You still must do it.)

Once the employer receives a report of discrimination or discriminatory harassment, they are supposed to conduct a reasonable investigation. If the discrimination or harassment has occurred, they must take prompt action to correct the situation. Plus, they're now on notice that an employee has a propensity toward illegal behavior.

With a little preparation and backbone, this meeting may help make your work life peaceful again. Here are some do's and don'ts for that meeting.

Do:

❑ Put your complaint in writing if you haven't already. Make sure you call it a "Formal Complaint of Racial [or Sexual/Age-Based/National Origin, etc.] Harassment [or Discrimination]." That way they can't claim later you only reported general harassment or bullying.

❑ Make notes to take with you. Write everything said or done where you were singled out for harassment or different treatment due to race, age, sex, national origin, pregnancy, color, genetic information, religion, or other protected status.

❑ If any comments were made about your protected status, write those down, too.

❑ Were you denied a raise, paid less, denied a promotion, or disciplined when others in a different category (different race, different sex, younger, non-disabled, etc.) were treated better? Write it down.

❑ Try to recall dates, who did it, witnesses, and any details. If you don't recall exact dates, it's okay to write "around May" or "last Spring." Do your best.

❑ List the names of everyone in your same category (same race, same sex, etc.) who was also treated badly.

❑ List the names of everyone in a different category from you who was treated better.

❑ If you have written proof (e-mails, memos, photos, recordings (not illegal tape recordings of conversations), or other documents), gather them to bring to the meeting. Be organized. You'll be more believable and look professional.

❑ Take good notes of the questions asked and the answers you gave.

❏ If you have an attorney, let her know about the meeting. Although she may not be allowed to attend, she might ask if she can. At the very least, she might give you some tips on what to say and what to expect. Your lawyer may have her own do's and don'ts she wants to go over with you. If you're represented, the company attorney can't meet with you without your lawyer's permission.

❏ If you're a union member, tell your representative. He'll probably want to attend.

❏ Stick to your guns. If they try to get you to change your story, to say it wasn't due to race/age/sex, etc. but something else, don't cave.

❏ Ask if you can see the investigative report once it's complete.

❏ If you remember something after the meeting, think you didn't have an opportunity to present everything, or want to clarify anything, write a memorandum to the people who attended laying out the details you want to add, so you have proof.

Don't:

❏ Don't tell coworkers about your complaint or bad-mouth anyone. Your complaint is supposed to be confidential. You might be disciplined for violating confidentiality.

❏ Don't mention unfair treatment, general harassment, personality conflicts, or bullying. Those aren't illegal. Focus on your complaint.

❏ Don't use illegal recordings. If you recorded a conversation with your harasser and the harasser didn't consent, in some states you may have committed a crime.

❏ Don't insist on having an attorney present. Most companies won't allow you to bring an attorney to an internal investigation. If you refuse to cooperate, they'll have a defense to your claim, and they might deem you insubordinate.

❏ Don't concede that the person you're complaining about dislikes everyone. If you are asked why the discriminating person did something to you, the answer is almost always: "Because of my race/age/sex/and so forth" or "To retaliate against me for reporting discrimination." If you say it's because they're a bully, you're giving the legal department ammunition to say the person is an "equal opportunity harasser" who is mean to everyone.

❑ Don't be evasive or try to play word games. You'll look like a liar.

❑ Don't ask for severance. They'll claim you quit. If they ask what you want, say you want to work in a place free of discrimination/sexual harassment/racial harassment/and so on. Don't quit. If they fire you, contact a lawyer.

❑ Don't demand the harasser be fired. They don't have to discipline this person in any particular way. Don't let them say that they have nowhere to put you in light of your demands.

❑ Don't yell, be insubordinate, be rude, or act unprofessionally. You'll give them a legitimate reason to fire you.

❑ Don't refuse to come back to work. They'll say you abandoned your position.

❑ Don't forget that HR and the corporate attorney are there to protect your employer, not you. Don't say or do anything that could get you disciplined or fired.

❑ Don't give the company your only copy of anything. Make copies of your notes, evidence, witness lists, etc.

❑ Don't freak out when they interview coworkers. They're supposed to. They must investigate. That means the harasser will probably find out about your complaint.

❑ Don't get upset if they say they won't give you a copy of the investigative report or let you know their conclusions. Some employers will; some won't. If you end up having to sue, the EEOC and your lawyer will be able to get the report.

❑ Don't be surprised if they conclude there was no discrimination or illegal harassment. Few HR people or lawyers will admit anything in writing. Even if the official report says it didn't happen, the harasser might have been warned or disciplined.

Once the interview is done, be patient. If you encounter more discrimination/discriminatory harassment, or if you are retaliated against, report it in writing to HR.

⊃ Most employers take discrimination complaints seriously and try to do the right thing. If you go into your meeting prepared, have proof and witness lists organized, act professionally, and don't have unreasonable expectations, this is your best opportunity to assure you have a workplace free of discrimination and discriminatory harassment.

⊃ If your employer doesn't correct the situation and it continues, or you are retaliated against by a demotion, termination, cut in pay/hours, or something that affects you in the wallet, it's time to talk to an employment attorney in your state.

⊃ The work you did to prepare for your meeting wasn't wasted. You'll be ready for your meeting with the lawyer. Hopefully you'll have enough ammunition to convince the attorney they can sue your employer's socks off.

Should I File a Grievance?

If you have a union, you likely have a grievance process. Some non-union employers have grievance processes set up for employees to address issues such as challenging discipline, discrimination, and anything affecting terms and conditions of employment.

If you have a grievance process, make sure you understand the deadlines for each step. If you miss any step, you'll lose your right to have your grievance heard.

If you have been disciplined or fired and there's nothing illegal like discrimination, the grievance may be your only remedy for general unfair treatment.

⊃ Some courts find failure to use the grievance process means an employee who sues the employer hasn't "exhausted remedies." This gives the court an excuse to throw out the case. On the other hand, if you raise an issue like discrimination and lose at the grievance level, some courts might say you've already litigated the issue so you can't go to court—sort of a catch-22. Other courts aren't allowing this type of "gotcha," so be aware of how the courts are handling this issue in your state. When in doubt, check with your union or a labor lawyer who handles union grievances.

⊃ If you have a union shop, I suggest joining it and getting active. Sometimes unions can decide whether or not to proceed with your grievance. If you're not a member, they won't push it for you. If you aren't happy with the union, run to be a union representative or officer. The only way to change things is to fight from within.

My Boss Is Creating a Hostile Environment. Can I Sue?

A hostile work environment is not illegal. Being a jerk or a bully is not illegal. If you complain about a hostile work environment or harassment, your employer can retaliate against you for complaining.

If the hostile environment is due to a protected status like race, age, sex, religion, national origin, genetic information, color, pregnancy, whistle-blowing, making a workers' comp claim, or objecting to safety violations, then you should follow the steps I address in the section in this chapter titled "I'm Being Bullied and Harassed. Can I Sue? on page 113."

If you, along with or on behalf of at least one coworker, report a supervisor who is making working conditions intolerable, you may be protected from retaliation under the National Labor Relations Act.

Donna's Tips

⊃ If the hostile environment is based on a protected status, you can and should complain in writing. Focus only on how you were treated as opposed to those who are in a different category.

⊃ Give the employer a chance to fix an illegal hostile environment.

⊃ If your boss is a bully or a jerk, look for another job. Don't quit until you find something else.

My Boss Hates Me Because We Have a Personality Conflict. Can I Sue?

There is absolutely nothing the law can do to help if your boss simply doesn't like you because you're you. Lower-level employees almost always lose personality conflicts. Here are some situations where a personality conflict might be something more:

Discrimination: Are you being singled out for worse treatment than other coworkers of a different race, age, sex, religion, national origin, or color? Did the boss's problem with you begin after you revealed your pregnancy, disability, or genetic information? Then the personality conflict might be due to discrimination. That's illegal. Keep notes of how you are being singled out compared to others in a different category.

Medical Leave: If you took FMLA leave and came back to a personality conflict, it might be Family and Medical Leave retaliation.

Whistle-Blowing: If you objected to or refused to participate in illegal activity of the company (as opposed to a coworker's illegal activities against the company), or after reporting the company's illegal activity to a government agency, then you might be suffering whistle-blower retaliation.

Concerted Activity: If you report a jerk boss making working conditions intolerable, and you are acting with or on behalf of coworkers, you may be protected from retaliation under the National Labor Relations Act.

Other Protected Status: If you've done anything recently that might put you in a protected status, such as testifying under subpoena, making a workers' compensation claim, or some other protected activity, and it was only after that when the personality conflict developed, you might have a retaliation claim.

Donna's Tips

⊃   If you're in a protected category and the personality conflict developed after your boss found out about your protected status or the boss is new, keep notes of how you're being singled out. After a few well-documented instances, report it to HR, in writing. Mention your protected status and how you are being singled out compared to others who aren't in your category.

⊃ If it's just a personality conflict, lay low and don't complain. You will lose. Try not to get into disputes with your boss. Follow instructions to the letter.

⊃ Do some CYA. If you think you're being set up, and you know you're being told to do something wrong, write an e-mail or memo to the boss. Repeat the instruction and state that you are confirming it. Ask her to advise immediately if this is not the instruction she wants you to follow.

I've Been Working for a Year and My Company Wants Me to Sign a Contract. Can They Make Me Do That?

Probably, yes. A majority of states still say continued employment is enough consideration to support a contract, such as a non-compete or non-solicitation contract. The theory is that, because your employment is at-will (that is, you can be fired for any reason or no reason at all), the employer can fire you for refusing to sign a contract, no matter how restrictive or ridiculous.

Some states require them to offer a promotion, more pay, or a bonus in order to require you to sign.

Even if your employer can make you sign, they probably can't get away with having you sign if they already know you are going to be fired or laid off. That would be fraud. It is information they should have disclosed to you before you signed.

Donna's Tips

⊃ If you are asked to sign a non-compete agreement or other contract, understand what you are agreeing to. Anyone who tells you that they are never enforced is mistaken or lying.

⊃ If you don't understand, ask for time to take it to an attorney to review. Even if you have no choice but to sign or be fired, it is best to understand before you sign. In some cases, you might be better off getting fired.

⊃ If you decide not to sign, let them fire you. Don't quit. You might lose unemployment if you do. Plus, some employers will threaten but won't actually fire top performers.

I Was Threatened at Work. Should I Complain to HR?

It depends on the threat. If a coworker, customer, or supervisor threatens to harm you (or your loved ones), definitely report it, in writing. The employer has a duty to maintain a safe workplace. Once you report it, if they don't take action to protect you and something happens, the company may be liable.

That's small comfort if you think you're really in danger. Unless you think the threat is life-threatening, I suggest you go back to work and try to avoid being alone with the person who threatens you. If the person makes other threats or lays hands on you, go back to HR.

If the threat is just to fire you or discipline you, then you probably must tough it out. Your boss can tell you this and there's nothing illegal about it.

Donna's Tips

- ⊃ If anyone physically harms you or you feel seriously threatened, call the police and file a report. You might even need to get a restraining order.

- ⊃ If you've exhausted all your options and think you aren't safe, by all means quit. No job is worth your safety.

A Coworker Shoved Me. Can I Shove Her Back?

Someone takes a swing at you or shoves you at work. You can defend yourself, right? Wrong. Most employers will fire both of you. I've seen people who only put their hands up to fend off blows who were fired. It all depends on whether or not they believe you. If they don't know who to believe, you're gone.

Remember: You're probably an at-will employee. Your employer does not have to get your firing right or be fair. They can fire you for any reason or no reason at all.

If a coworker, supervisor, or customer attacks you, then you have a quick decision to make. My suggestion is drop to the floor and curl in a fetal position. Cover your face and scream as loud as you can for help. It's hard for the other person to claim they're the victim if they're on top of you.

If you're alone, do what you must do to defend yourself. Just realize that you might be fired. Report the incident to HR and the police as soon as possible.

Donna's Tips

- ⊃ I've even seen people fired because they called the police. In most states, they can fire you for that. Still, if you are a crime victim it's best to involve the police.

- ⊃ The attack can be turned back on you. The attacker can and probably will claim you were the aggressor. If you have witnesses, make sure they're willing to back you up.

- ⊃ If you report an attack to HR and they can't protect you, don't work in a dangerous situation. Get out of there as soon as you can, even though you'll lose your job.

Does My Company Have to Cover Me With Workers' Compensation?

Most employers are required to have workers' compensation insurance, but not all. Workers' compensation is governed by state law, so requirements will depend on which state you live in. Some exemptions exist for very small employers, for instance. Other exemptions may be in certain industries or job classifications in your state, such as independent contractors, agricultural workers, relatives of owners, domestic employees, and realtors. In dangerous industries, such as construction, workers' compensation coverage is almost always required.

The effect of not having workers' compensation insurance is that employers can be sued directly for workplace injuries. Covered employers are not liable for injuries at work, with few exceptions. Employers who fail to obtain coverage may also be subject to civil or criminal penalties.

Donna's Tips

- ⊃ If you're in a dangerous profession, make sure the employer carries workers' compensation insurance.

- ⊃ If you are injured at work, report your injury immediately, and make sure the employer fills out the paperwork to report your claim. If you find out you're injured after the fact, report it as soon as you know about it. If you don't report it, you might lose coverage.

- ⊃ It is illegal to fire you for making a workers' compensation claim.

Scenarios on Discipline, Coworkers, Bullies, and Harassment

Scenario 1

Your boss calls you for a meeting. When you arrive, your boss is at the head of the table with a woman you've never met. The woman introduces herself as the head of human resources. You're presented with a written warning. When you read it, you're stunned. It's all untrue! The HR lady says you must sign it. Do you:

❏ a. Say, "No way. I'm not signing this. It's all untrue."?

❏ b. Demand to know who told them all this? Tell them you have a right to confront your accusers. "You should fire them. They're liars!"

❏ c. Sign, "As to receipt only, written rebuttal to follow."? Tell them calmly you disagree with the information in the warning and you will work on a response.

If you answered a:

Lots of employees refuse to sign disciplinary notices. Whether it's a counseling, warning, written reprimand, or suspension, anything before you're terminated is something you should sign. Why? Because refusing an order to sign it just might be considered insubordination. It also makes you look like a.) a jerk; b.) unprofessional; or c.) like you don't know what you are doing. Refusing to sign doesn't make it go away. They'll probably write on it: "Refused to sign." That looks good come promotion time, doesn't it?

If you answered b:

The right to confront your accusers applies in criminal court, not in the workplace. Many times, your coworkers are protected by your employer's confidentiality policy for reporting what they believe is wrongdoing. Don't start insulting your accuser. They could be your boss's most trusted confidant, the HR lady's cousin, or the CEO's daughter. Name-calling makes you look unprofessional and won't accomplish anything except convince HR and your boss that you're volatile and irrational.

If you answered c:

You may save your job. Always get a copy of everything you sign. Take it home, where you can review it calmly. Then prepare your rebuttal. Be factual; this is not the time to insult your boss, complain about professionalism, or air general grievances. Be specific about what is untrue in the document. If you have proof, attach it. If you have witnesses, list them (but remember that most coworkers will lie to save their jobs, no matter how much you think they're your friends).

If you were treated differently than others of a different race, age, sex, religion, color, national origin, genetic information; who wasn't disabled or pregnant; or who hadn't recently taken FMLA leave, made a workers' comp claim, or objected to illegal activity (in other words, if you were you singled out due to some legally protected status), now is the time to point that out.

Scenario 2

Same as scenario 1, except the HR lady says, "We've decided to terminate your employment, effective immediately." She hands you a form and tells you to sign. Do you:

- ❑ a. Say: "No way. I'm not signing this. It's all untrue."?
- ❑ b. Sign, "As to receipt only, written rebuttal to follow."?
  Tell them calmly you disagree with the information in the termination form and you will work on a response.
- ❑ c. Say, "I'd like to take a copy of this so I can review it."?

If you answered a:

This is fine, assuming you aren't being offered anything. You're already gone. Why should you cooperate with anything the now-former employer wants you to do?

If you answered b:

You are probably wasting your time preparing a rebuttal. They've made up their minds. I suggest signing "as to receipt only" if they offer severance, offer positive references, or say they won't challenge your unemployment. If they offer a severance package, then get a copy of the form and the proposed severance package (which you should not sign yet), and take them to a lawyer to review. If the employer offers positive references and/or says they won't challenge your unemployment, sign the form, "as to receipt only," and get a copy of the form.

If you answered c:

This is a good answer. You're shaken and aren't thinking straight. Always get a copy of the termination papers, whether or not you sign. You may need this to prove to unemployment that you were fired— and if you think you have potential claims, your lawyer will want to see it. If they won't give them to you, don't argue.

Scenario 3

You've reported sexual harassment to HR. You get a call from the VP of human resources. The company attorney and he want to meet with you to interview you about your complaint. Do you:

❑ a. Refuse to meet? You have the right to remain silent.

❑ b. Refuse to meet unless you have your lawyer present?

❑ c. Panic? "I need more time. Can we meet next month?"

❑ d. Say, "Thank you. Let me know when and where."? Then work on gathering evidence to take with you.

If you answered a:

You've been watching too many criminal law TV shows. The right to remain silent applies to criminal investigations by the police, not to an investigation by HR that you initiated. If you refuse to meet, they will assume you are lying. It won't be much of an investigation, and failing to cooperate with the investigation might be a defense for the company if you sue later.

If you answered b:

They probably won't let you have a lawyer present at an internal company meeting. If you ask politely whether your lawyer may attend, they may agree but don't have to. If you aren't allowed to have a lawyer present, take good notes so you can show your lawyer later.

If you answered c:

Some employees refuse or delay, but this meeting is a good sign. They're investigating. By delaying the meeting, you may force them to do the investigation without you. It's better to give your side first so they know what to ask other witnesses and what evidence to gather.

If you answered d:

Good for you! Now get ready. Make notes to take. List any sexual comments, overtures, dates, details, witnesses, and what they witnessed. You will seem more credible in the meeting.

Scenario 4

Your boss is a yeller. He screams, leaning over 6 inches from your face. He curses, throws things around the room, and creates a hostile environment for you and everyone in your office. Do you:

❑ a. Report him to HR? Explain how he's creating a hostile work environment and give them an opportunity to correct the situation.

❑ b. File with the EEOC?

❑ c. Quit and then contact an employment lawyer to sue the company?

❑ d. Suck it up and start looking for another job?

If you answered a:

You can do this, but know that you aren't protected if the boss retaliates. There is no legal requirement that the company deal with bullying. However, some companies won't tolerate it.

If you answered b:

They will, hopefully politely, tell you that they do not deal with bullying.

If you answered c:

Never, ever quit your job without having another job lined up (unless your safety or mental health is at risk). You just gave the bully what he wanted and put yourself in a terrible situation. His bullying isn't illegal, so the lawyer will probably tell you there's nothing you can do. To top it off, you might not even qualify for unemployment in some states.

If you answered d:

Smart move. Don't let a bully force you out of a job. Quit only when you have something else lined up. In the meantime, try to stay out of his way.

Scenario 5

Same as scenario 4, except he's only picking on you. It started right after you returned from your maternity leave. Do you:

- ❑ a. Report him to HR? Explain how he's creating a hostile work environment and give them an opportunity to correct the situation.
- ❑ b. File with the EEOC?
- ❑ c. Quit and then contact an employment lawyer to sue the company?
- ❑ d. Suck it up and start looking for another job?

If you answered a:

That's your right move, except you must say that it's hostile due to your having taken FMLA leave. If your leave was due to pregnancy or a disability, then also say that the environment is hostile due to pregnancy/disability. Put your complaint in writing so you have proof you did it.

If you answered b:

You skipped a step. If the company has a published harassment policy, you must report it first and give them a chance to correct the situation. If they don't fix it, or if you're retaliated against, it might be time to go to the EEOC.

If you answered c:

You played right into the harasser's hands. He wanted you gone and you're gone. By not complaining under the policy, you might have given up your right to sue.

If you answered d:

You're not wrong to get out of there. However, by skipping step a, you've likely given up your right to sue.

Scenario 6

Your coworker plays loud music all day long. It's distracting. It makes work difficult. You have trouble concentrating. Do you:

- ❑ a. Complain to your boss?

❑ b. Ask the coworker nicely to turn the music down (or off)?

❑ c. File a grievance with HR?

If you answered a:

Your boss might be the one to speak with a difficult coworker. However, if the boss is friendly with the coworker, you might be retaliated against. That won't be illegal. You might buy a noise cancellation headset and deal with the issue yourself.

If you answered b:

If the coworker isn't nuts or on a power trip, then this will probably work. If they refuse, you might need to go to the boss. However, retaliation isn't illegal. Tread carefully.

If you answered c:

This is probably a mistake. You've gone over your boss's head, and haven't even spoken to your coworker. Plus, the grievance policy, if it exists at all, is probably for violations of the union contract, not for petty complaints against coworkers.

Scenario 7

Same as scenario 6, except the loud music started after you admitted to your coworker that you are of Arab descent. You've tried asking nicely, and she says, "Why don't you have Allah make me?" Do you:

❑ a. Go to HR and complain about religious and national origin harassment?

❑ b. Ignore it and hope it will stop?

❑ c. Bring in your own MP3 player and play loud Arabic music just to annoy them back?

If you answered a:

This is the smart play. The harassment is related to your religion and national origin, so you must report it under the harassment policy. Make sure that HR is the right place to go under the policy. Put the complaint in writing.

If you answered b:

It's possible it will stop, but it's also possible the coworker will accelerate the behavior and it will get worse.

If you answered c:

You're probably both fired. Don't make the situation worse. Your boss will hate you for it. "He started it" didn't work with your parents and it certainly won't work in the office.

Scenario 8

Your boss is an incompetent fool. She doesn't take your suggestions, doesn't know anything about her job, and is a terrible supervisor. Do you:

- ❏ a. Write a long letter detailing this idiot's incompetence and suggestions for how she can do her job better?
- ❏ b. Try to get along with her? Do your work the best you can. If she tells you to do something you know is wrong, confirm the instruction in writing.
- ❏ c. Quit? It's impossible to work like this.

If you answered a:

Why, why, why? Tell me you didn't hit "send." Although the letter might be cathartic to write, if you send it you will be retaliated against and will be treated as a pariah. You probably have zero promotional opportunities and may be fired.

If you answered b:

Smart cookie! If she's that bad, eventually the powers that be will catch up to her (unless she's someone's niece). Work your best despite her, and hope she's gone soon.

If you answered c:

Great. Now you have no job and probably don't qualify for unemployment. I hope you have lots of savings.

Scenario 9

You've been working six months. Your boss hands you a document and says, "I need you to sign this today." You look and it's called, "Confidentiality Agreement." Do you:

- ❏ a. Sign it? Sounds harmless.
- ❏ b. Ask if you can have time to take it to an attorney to review?
- ❏ c. Refuse to sign? They can't make you sign anything after you started because there's no consideration for the contract.

If you answered a:

You might have just signed an agreement that you won't work for a competitor for a year or two. I hope you don't mind starting over in a new industry after you leave.

If you answered b:

If you don't understand what you're signing, then definitely get legal advice. Never sign anything if you can't live with it.

If you answered c:

In all but a few states, continued employment is valid consideration for a contract. That means they can say, "Sign or be fired." In some states, an agreement signed that way might not be enforceable. Still, you can probably be fired for not signing.

Scenario 10

Your coworker doesn't like you. You try to work, but he constantly makes negative comments and tries to sabotage you. One day, he says, "I'm going to get you fired if it's the last thing I do." Do you:

❏ a. Report this to your boss? It's harassment.

❏ b. Make sure you document everything? Write down his comments and keep your records at home. If you catch him in actual sabotage, go to the boss and report it, with your evidence.

❏ c. Sue the company for hostile environment?

❏ d. Call the police? He threatened you.

If you answered a:

You may be able to report it and have the boss do something about it. However, this type of harassment is not illegal. If you report it, you aren't protected from retaliation. Be careful.

If you answered b:

It's definitely a good idea to keep track of the comments and get evidence of any actual sabotage. Reporting your suspicions is one thing, but reporting probable sabotage might get the boss's attention. This type of harassment is not illegal, so you're not protected from retaliation.

If you answered c:

Sorry. A hostile environment is not illegal.

If you answered d:

Sorry. The police won't handle a threat to cost you a job. They deal with physical threats only, and rarely with any threats unless you're physically harmed.

Scenario 11

Same as scenario 10, except he's made it clear he resents working with a woman. His comments include anti-female comments and name-calling that rhymes with "witch," and his threat is that he'll follow you to your car one night and slash your throat. Do you:

- ❑ a. Call the police?
- ❑ b. Report him to your boss and HR for sexual harassment and workplace violence?
- ❑ c. Quit? You can't work like this.

If you answered a:

You're not wrong to do this. He made a physical threat of violence. If you're truly scared, it might not be a bad idea to file a police report and get it on record. However, some employers will fire you for filing a police report on a coworker. They would prefer to handle it internally.

If you answered b:

If the company has a published sexual harassment policy, then this is where you should go. Report it to whomever the company designates in the policy. Put the complaint in writing. List all the anti-female comments and name-calling. State that he threatened you, and you believe he would not treat a male this way. Ask that they take prompt action to correct the situation. In the meantime, make sure you are never alone with this person and have someone walk with you to your car, especially at night.

If you answered c:

If you're truly scared, this might be an option. But think about the consequences: You've let him win. He got rid of you, which is what he wanted. You're unemployed and in a terrible financial situation. Plus, you've lost your right to sue for sexual harassment. You've probably lost your entitlement to unemployment. No job is worth risking your life, but it's better to try to get some help first before you quit. In the meantime, you can start looking for another job and get out of there on your own terms if the company doesn't fix the problem.

Scenario 12

Same as scenario 10, except he traps you in the file room. When you try to get past, he shoves you and calls you a name. Do you:

❑ a. Shove him back? He can't treat you like this.

❑ b. Yell for help?

❑ c. Pull out your cell phone? Take a picture. Call 911 if he won't move.

If you answered a:

Bad move. Once you fight back, you're probably both fired. Odds are, someone will walk past and see you do it, but they didn't see him. You could be fired and not him.

If you answered b:

Probably the right move. If nobody is around, you might have to do choice c. If he tries to harm you, then you should do anything you must do in self-defense (but know that you'll likely lose your job over it).

If you answered c:

This may work if other people are around. It might intimidate him into backing off. You'll have proof that he blocked you in (sort of). You could call 911, or drop to the ground, curl in a fetal position with your hands in front of your face and elbows at ribs to protect yourself, and yell. There's no great answer for this problem when you have an attacker who denies he attacked you and there are no witnesses.

Scenario 13

You're hurt at work when you slam your finger into a file cabinet. It's embarrassing, but you think it might be serious. Do you:

❑ a. Ignore it? You're too embarrassed to report it. Maybe it will be okay.

❑ b. Report it to HR or whoever handles workers' compensation injuries?

❑ c. Go to your own doctor to have her look at it?

f you answered a:

It might go away, but if you don't report it then you might lose any possible workers' compensation coverage. If you think you're injured, it's best to report it as soon as the injury happens. Some companies will even discipline you for failing to report an injury.

If you answered b:

In most companies, this is the right move. Some will fire you for making a workers' comp claim, but that is illegal. At least you'll be covered if the injury turns out to be serious.

If you answered c:

If you tell a doctor the injury happened at work, you may not be covered by your medical insurance. That means you might be stuck with the whole medical bill for your injury.

5 Good Stuff Happens:

Promotions, New Contracts

Got a Promotion. Does That Mean They Must Pay Me More?

There is no law requiring employers to pay you more just because you got promoted. Sometimes a better job title means less pay because you're exempt from overtime. Once you're exempt (assuming you're really exempt), you can be required to work ridiculous hours for no extra pay.

If you decline a promotion, you can be fired. Many times, employers will hold it against you if you say no. They take it as an insult. However, if your promotion means a pay cut you can't afford, say no if you can.

Sometimes, a promotion resulting in a pay cut means more opportunity for advancement. Weigh the pluses and minuses, and the impact on your wallet when considering any promotion.

Donna's Tips

➭ Ask about pay before you accept. Also ask if it will make you exempt from overtime if you are used to being paid overtime and rely on the extra income.

➭ Just because they call you "salaried exempt" doesn't make it so. If you're doing the same duties for less pay and a fancy title, you may still be non-exempt and entitled to overtime.

➭ Don't be so flattered by a "promotion" that you forget to ask the big questions before you accept.

Now That I'm a Supervisor, They Say They Don't Have to Pay Overtime. Is That True?

It's very possible you are now exempt from overtime. It mostly depends on your job duties. Assuming you make $23,600 or more and are salaried, here are the supervisory-type job duties that will make you exempt:

Executive Duties: You're exempt if you supervise two or more employees, management is your primary job, and you have genuine input into the hiring, promotion, and firing of your subordinates.

Administrative Duties: If you perform office or non-manual work that's directly related to management or the general business operations of your company or their customers, and are regularly required to use your independent judgment and discretion about significant matters, you might be exempt. An administrative assistant who is the right hand to the CEO is probably exempt, but the secretary to a mid-level manager probably isn't.

Donna's Tips

- If you make less than $23,600 ($455/week), you're never exempt.

- If your employer docks your pay when you miss part of the workday, you're not exempt. But they can deduct paid time off from your leave bank if you miss work.

- If you're exempt, they can't dock you if there is no work or if work is slow.

- You can be docked for missed full days due to disciplinary suspension, sick days, or personal leave even if you're exempt.

- Even if you're salaried, you're still not exempt from overtime unless you also have exempt job duties.

They Handed Me a Contract to Sign to Get My Promotion. Should I Sign?

Sure, go ahead and sign without reading. You're management. They wouldn't mess with you now, would they? Ha! Wrong, wrong, wrong. Read it carefully, and understand it before you sign, as with any other contract. Now that you're management, they are more concerned about what information you have access to and whether or not you work for a competitor.

Some provisions to watch out for are:

Non-Compete: You may be agreeing not to work in your industry for a year or two after you cease working for this employer. Watch out for the length, industries covered, and geographic area where you are restricted.

Confidentiality: With this clause, you agree keep the employer's confidential information to yourself. Don't let the name "Confidentiality Agreement" fool you, though. Sometimes employers sneak in non-compete language or other restrictions. Read them carefully.

Non-Solicitation: You're agreeing not to solicit the company's customers or employees to go to another company. Have a book of business? It might be the company's property if you sign.

Intellectual Property: You're agreeing that anything you thought of, designed, created, wrote, or conceived of while you were employed belongs to them. If you write novels, paint, design video games, sketch doll designs, or do anything creative, negotiate an exclusion.

> **Donna's Tips**

- ⊃ When in doubt, have a lawyer review any new employment agreement before you sign.

- ⊃ If you know you'll have to sign an agreement in order to be promoted, ask for a copy to review before you accept. If you can't live with the agreement, either negotiate before you sign or decline the promotion.

- ⊃ If they want you in the position badly enough, you have leverage to negotiate. But if there's someone else who could take the job if you pass, you will probably have to take it or leave it. Still, it never hurts to try to negotiate the worst provisions if you want the promotion. If they say no, you may have to take a pass.

Now That I'm Management, Could I Be Personally Liable for Something the Company Does?

With great power comes great responsibility. Yes, you could be sued personally for something you do as a manager. Here are some laws that you should be aware of to make sure you aren't on the losing end of a lawsuit:

Fair Labor Standards Act: Get it wrong on overtime pay, who is exempt, minimum wage, timekeeping, or docking, and you may be personally liable. If you are involved in decisions relating to anything covered by FLSA, get it right.

Equal Pay Act: Unlike Title VII, you might have personal liability if you fail to pay equal wages for equivalent work.

Family and Medical Leave Act (FMLA): The courts have been mixed on this. Depending on what circuit you live in, you may have personal exposure if you deny FMLA leave or retaliate against someone for taking medical leave.

Consolidated Omnibus Budget Reconciliation Act (COBRA): Individual decision-makers can be liable for COBRA violations.

Section 1983 of the Civil Rights Act: You could be held personally liable for discrimination under the federal civil rights statute covering race discrimination.

Employee Retirement Income Security Act (ERISA): If you are the person responsible for making contributions to pension plans or deciding who is eligible, or have other fiduciary responsibilities, you might be liable under ERISA.

Occupational Safety and Health Act (OSHA): If you order employees to go into unsafe situations or don't make sure the workplace is safe, you may have personal liability for OSHA violations.

Immigration Reform and Control Act: If you knowingly hire illegal aliens, or look the other way, Homeland Security may want to speak with you. You could have both civil and criminal liability.

Tort Claims: In defamation, battery, assault, intentional infliction of emotional distress, privacy, negligent hiring and supervision, fraud, and other tort cases, you can be sued personally, especially if what you did was outside the scope of your employment. You don't have to be a manager to get sued for torts you commit.

State Law Claims: Some state discrimination laws hold managers personally liable for discrimination committed under their watch.

In most states you will not be personally liable under the following:

Title VII of the Civil Rights Act of 1964: All but one federal circuit say there is no individual liability under Title VII for discrimination.

Americans with Disabilities Act (ADA): Most circuits say there is no individual liability for violations of the Americans with Disabilities Act.

Age Discrimination in Employment Act: Most circuits find there is no individual liability under the Age Discrimination in Employment Act.

Donna's Tips

➲ Beware of a "go along to get along" attitude. If the company is breaking the law, you may have personal responsibility to make sure they don't do it under your watch or your instructions.

➲ If you are fired for objecting to or refusing to participate in illegal practices, you might be a protected whistle-blower.

➲ Just because it's always been done that way, doesn't mean they've done it right. Understand the laws applying to your managerial responsibilities and get it right.

Crisis Scenarios for New Promotions

Scenario 1

You get called into HR. You go in trembling, scared you're in trouble. But it's good news—great news, in fact. You've been promoted! Do you:

❑ a. Say, "Wow, what an honor!"? Beam, shake their hand, and call your spouse to chill some champagne.

❑ b. Thank them for the honor? Ask about your new job duties and any pay changes. Ask for a day or two to think about it before you accept, especially if there's something you don't understand.

❑ c. Yell, "Yippee!" then run out to the desk of your most hated coworker, and say, "Suck it! I'm your new boss. Deal with it, jerk."?

If you answered a:

Celebrate if you already know everything you should know about the job: whether you're exempt from overtime, whether you still get commissions, if your hours will change, who you'll be supervising, and whether or not you must sign a contract. If you don't know the answers to these concerns, you may be getting into more than you bargained for, such as a pay cut, a non-compete agreement, crazy hours, or even a new job location.

If you answered b:

You're handling this the smart way. You are being professional, asking relevant questions about the new job, and not jumping into anything. While some companies will give you a hard time if you turn down a promotion, many will respect a decision to stay where you are. Understand whether or not this will be a good move before you leap.

If you answered c:

If HR hasn't changed their mind immediately, you are still off to a bad start with your unprofessionalism. You probably won't be a supervisor for long. Plus, you don't have the relevant information you need to make a good decision to accept or not.

Scenario 2

You're offered a promotion. You've done your research and have decided being a supervisor isn't for you. You tell HR you've respectfully decided to decline the position. They say, "We've already filled your position and don't have anywhere else to put you. If you don't take it, you're fired." Do you:

❑ a. Take it? It's better than being unemployed.

❑ b. Hand in your resignation?

❑ c. Tell them you'll take it? Then start looking at options. Talk to someone who has held the position. Look for openings elsewhere.

If you answered a:

This may be your only choice for the moment. But do explore your options. Choice c is your better choice unless you must sign a non-compete agreement right away. If they shove one in front of you and order you to sign, ask to take it to a lawyer to review. If they say no, you might have to sign or be fired.

If you answered b:

This is the smart move only if you must sign a non-compete agreement, non-solicitation agreement, or other agreement you can't live with and that will limit your ability to look elsewhere. Otherwise, take the job and start looking for something else while you're employed.

If you answered c:

This is your best bet if you aren't signing away your options by accepting. Who knows? It may work out in the new position. Or you may find something better outside the company. Having a better job title might open up some opportunities.

Scenario 3

You've accepted a promotion, thinking it will be great. You end up working 60 hours a week with no overtime. In your old job you got overtime and commissions. You were making more before you were promoted. Do you:

- ❑ a. Ask about being allowed to step down to your old position level?
- ❑ b. Look around internally for another position with better pay and less crazy hours?
- ❑ c. Start looking for something outside the company?

If you answered a:

Some companies will allow this and be understanding. Promotions aren't for everyone. If you know the corporate culture doesn't punish people who do this, it may be your best choice.

If you answered b:

Some companies make you stay in a new position for a minimum time, such as six months or a year, before they will let you move. If you are lucky enough not to have such a restriction, you may still have a lot of explaining to do about why you stayed such a short time in your new position. Still, this is one option to consider.

If you answered c:

This is another possible choice. Unlike the internal move, it may be subject to less scrutiny because you'll be able to show you were with your current employer for a long time. If you're asked how long you've held your position, you may still need to explain why you're leaving after such a short time. Just be careful you know what you're getting into in the new company before you jump. Try not to burn bridges if you leave. Give plenty of notice and do what you can to smooth the transition for your successor.

Scenario 4

You've been promoted to a position called "supervisor," but it's really just your old job with a bigger salary. You don't get overtime anymore. You don't supervise anyone, but now you are expected to work evenings and weekends. Do you:

❑ a. Ask to be paid overtime and point out to them that your duties and job description mean you're not exempt?

❑ b. Ask to step down to your old position.

❑ c. Start looking for another job?

If you answered a:

This might work if they are reasonable. If they aren't, then they might retaliate (which is illegal, but that doesn't help while you're there). If they say no, you should contact the Department of Labor or an employment lawyer who handles wage and hour cases to see what your rights are.

If you answered b:

This probably won't work. You're already in your old position. They just don't want to pay overtime anymore. If they do let you do it, breathe a sigh of relief and hope they don't retaliate.

If you answered c:

Definitely, especially if you've tried choice a or b. These people are jerks, and they're breaking the law. You should get out of there, then contact Department of Labor or a lawyer about collecting the overtime pay you're owed.

Scenario 5

You've worked for a month as a supervisor. Your boss hands you a thick document and says, "Here's the contract for your promotion. I need it back signed by the end of the day." Do you:

❑ a. Sign and hand it back to him?

❑ b. Tell him you would like some additional time to take it to your lawyer to review?

❑ c. Read it carefully, then hand it back with some notes of changes you would like?

If you answered a:

Surely you knew better. Is the air up in the executive suite too thin? You didn't even ask for a copy, did you? You probably signed an agreement that you won't work for a competitor for two years. If you design video games or are working on the Great American Novel in your spare time, they probably own it now. Why did they promote you again?

If you answered b:

It's best to get time to review it, with or without a lawyer. If you don't understand all the legalese, get a lawyer to review it with you. If the boss says, "Sign it now or be fired," you're in a tough situation. You should at least be allowed to read it. If you decide to sign, get a copy.

If you answered c:

If you know what you're doing and are good at negotiation, this may be the right decision. Many people are savvy enough to read, understand and negotiate their own contracts. Get a copy of the executed version. If they say, "Take it or leave it," you'll have a big decision to make.

Scenario 6

Same as scenario 5, except when you read it, your job title and salary are different than what you have now, and the change is not in your favor. Do you:

❑ a. Ask what's going on? Are you being demoted?

❑ b. Say, "I'm not signing this. I don't agree to the pay cut and job change."?

❑ c. Contact HR and ask if this is the right contract? If so, ask why the changes are being made.

If you answered a:

Good question. Your boss might or might not know. She's a good place to start.

If you answered b:

If the change is something you can't live with, you may have to do this. However, you might be fired if you refuse. Get more information first, and explore your corporate and legal options before you decide to do this.

If you answered c:

If your boss isn't someone you can talk to, or if she doesn't know the answer, HR is the place to go next. Find out if this is a demotion, is-something temporary, or if you were misled when you accepted the position.

Scenario 7

Your new position requires you to sign off on time sheets. Your instructions are to never authorize overtime. Yet your staff is working 55 hours a week and corporate knows this darned well. Do you:

- ❑ a. Alter the timesheets to show 8.0 hours a day?
- ❑ b. Find a way to cut staff hours? Look at hiring more staff if you can. In the meantime, sign timesheets reflecting the correct hours.
- ❑ c. Order your staff to never turn in a time sheet showing more than 8.0 hours a day upon pain of termination?

If you answered a:

You have broken the law, and are committing fraud on top of failing to pay for all hours worked. You are probably personally liable for this legal violation. Better check your insurance policy.

If you answered b:

This is the only way to go. If the powers-that-be threaten to fire you for doing it right, contact the Department of Labor or a lawyer about your rights and responsibilities.

If you answered c:

You're still breaking the law. You know they aren't working those hours. The fact that it's your staff submitting the false time records doesn't mean you won't be sued personally.

Scenario 8

As a supervisor, you become aware that some people working under you are getting paid cash. You discover they are illegal aliens, working off the books because they aren't authorized to work in the United States. Do you:

❑ a. Smile when you hand out the cash? Poor people, it's not their fault. You're glad to help.

❑ b. Object to and refuse to participate in this practice?

❑ c. Call Homeland Security and report the company?

If you answered a:

You may have a very uncomfortable conversation with Homeland Security if they raid the company and find out what is going on. You may have civil or criminal liability for participating in this.

If you answered b:

You absolutely must do this if you don't want to have to defend yourself in court later. If you do this, you're probably protected from retaliation as a whistle-blower.

If you answered c:

If you object and the company still insists on continuing this practice, you may have no choice but to report them. If you report this unlawful activity to Homeland Security and you haven't been involved in the practice, you should be a protected whistle-blower. If you did participate, get out of the company before all heck breaks loose.

Evidence Gathering:

What You Need to Prove Discrimination, Harassment, Whistle-Blowing

Can I Sue For Discrimination?

Discrimination against you because you're you isn't illegal. Favoritism, nepotism (except in some government entities), bullying, and unfair treatment aren't discrimination. Here's what you need to know about employment discrimination:

Protected Categories: Title VII of the Civil Rights Act of 1964 protects against race, sex, national origin, color, and religious discrimination. The Age Discrimination in Employment Act protects against age discrimination. The Americans with Disabilities Act protects against disability discrimination. The Pregnancy Discrimination Act adds pregnancy to Title VII's protections. The Genetic Information Nondiscrimination Act of 2008 protects against genetic information discrimination. Some states and local governments protect against other types of discrimination such as marital status, domestic violence victims, parental status, and sexual orientation.

Direct Evidence: In very few cases, supervisors will make comments that demonstrate their biases. I've even seen some cases where the termination letter says the reason for the firing is something protected, such as age. This is called direct evidence, and it's rare.

Other Evidence: If you've been treated differently under the same circumstances than coworkers in a different category, then you may be able to show discrimination. For example, if you were disciplined for making personal calls when everyone of a different sex was allowed to make personal calls freely, that might be sex discrimination. If a neutral practice like a promotional test has an adverse impact on one category of employees, then it could be discriminatory even if the practice applies to everyone. For example, a test where 90 percent of whites and only 5 percent of blacks passed might show race discrimination.

Harassment: If you haven't had anything happen that affects you in the wallet (as examples, demotion, firing, denial of a promotion, suspension without pay), then the discrimination falls in the category of harassment. Harassment based on race, age, sex, and so forth is illegal. But you must report the harassment to the company under its harassment policy first and give the company a chance to fix the situation.

Small Employers: If your employer has fewer than 15 employees, then it's allowed to discriminate. Yes, that's what I said. The only federal law that protects against discrimination by employers is 42 U.S.C. § 1981, which addresses only race, color, ancestry, and ethnic characteristics discrimination, and covers hiring, promotion, discharge, hostile environment, and retaliation. Some states, counties, and cities have laws protecting employees of smaller employers.

Donna's Tips

⊃ Be familiar with the company handbook, posters, and written policies. Don't wait until you're distraught from being harassed to figure out where you must report discriminatory harassment.

⊃ If you report illegal discrimination under the company policy, they're not allowed to retaliate. That doesn't mean they won't retaliate. If you're retaliated against, then either report the retaliation to HR or contact a lawyer.

⊃ Don't wait to pursue discrimination claims. They have short deadlines to act. When in doubt, consult an attorney.

How Do I Prove Discrimination and Harassment?

Many people are confused about what evidence they need to prove discrimination. There are several ways you can prove discrimination. It's not as hard as you think. What is discrimination? How do you prove it? And what do you do if you think you're a victim of discrimination? I'll give you some examples here.

Some Types of Discrimination

Age Discrimination

Age 40 and Older: It's illegal for an employer to discriminate against you because of your age. The Age Discrimination in Employment Act prohibits age discrimination only if you're age 40 or older, and only if the employer has at least 20 employees. Some states have laws that protect employees of smaller employers.

Younger Than 40: Some states have laws that prohibit discrimination based on being too old or too young.

Disability Discrimination

If you have an impairment that substantially limits a major life activity, you might be covered under the Americans with Disabilities Act (ADA). The impairment can be physical or mental. Homosexuality, pregnancy, weight, and height are not considered disabilities. The disability doesn't have to be permanent. Temporary impairments that take significantly longer than normal to heal, long-term impairments, or potentially long term impairments of indefinite duration may be disabilities if they are severe.

Major Life Activities: Examples are caring for yourself, performing manual tasks, walking, seeing, hearing, speaking, breathing, learning, working, sitting, standing, lifting, thinking, concentrating, and interacting with others.

Substantially Limiting: The disability must prohibit or significantly restrict your ability to perform a major life activity compared average people. Courts will weigh the nature and severity, the duration or expected duration, and the permanent or long-term impact of the impairment.

Ability to Work: The impairment substantially limits the ability to work if it prevents or significantly restricts you from performing a class of jobs or a broad range of jobs in various classes (as opposed to your specific job).

Record of Disability: Even if you aren't disabled currently, you might be protected if you have a record of disability. That means you either have a history of a substantially limiting impairment or have been misclassified as having a substantially limiting impairment.

Regarded as Disabled: If your employer regards you as disabled, then you're also protected against discrimination. If you have an impairment that doesn't substantially limit major life activities but your employer treats you as if you do; have an impairment that substantially limits major life activities only as a result of the attitudes of others toward your impairment; or have no impairment but your employer treats you as if you do, then you're covered. A good example of this is if your supervisor suddenly assumes you have AIDS because you lost weight.

Drug Addiction: You're not covered if you're currently using illegal drugs. If you have kicked the habit or the company only assumes you're an addict, you're protected.

Accommodation: If you need an accommodation in order to perform all the duties of your job, you should request it from your employer. They can't deny a reasonable accommodation unless it's an undue hardship.

Covered Employers: 15 or more employees, except age discrimination, which requires 20 employees. Even if you work for a smaller employer, race discrimination at work is also illegal under 42 U.S.C. Sec. 1981.

Race Discrimination

Discrimination based on your race includes discrimination based on characteristics associated with race, such as skin color, hair texture, or facial features as well as conditions that primarily affect one race (such as sickle cell anemia or severe shaving bumps in African-Americans).

Color Discrimination

Even if your harasser is the same race, you can still complain about discrimination if they're biased due to your color. Basically, color means the shade of your skin. If someone of your same race favors lighter- or darker-skinned employees, then that could be color discrimination.

Sex Discrimination

If you think you're being singled out for different treatment or harassment due to your gender, you might have a sex discrimination case.

National Origin Discrimination

National origin discrimination includes discrimination based on your national origin or your family's national origin. If you were born in the United States but your family is originally from, say, Saudi Arabia, you are protected from national origin discrimination. The EEOC considers harassment due to being Hispanic national origin rather than race discrimination. I suggest filing the charge as both just to be safe, because jurics and judges might view it differently.

English-Only Rules: In general, English-only rules in the workplace are allowed if they are enacted for non-discriminatory reasons. Examples of good reasons to have English-only rules would be because customers, supervisors, and coworkers speak only English; for workplace safety reasons such as emergencies where everyone needs to understand; to promote efficiency for cooperative assignments; and to allow supervisors who speak only English to monitor employees' communications with customers.

Examples of illegal policies are:

❯ Prohibiting non-English speaking on breaks.

❯ Subjecting speakers of foreign languages to excess scrutiny.

❯ Prohibiting one particular foreign language from being spoken.

❯ Requiring English-only if coworkers and customers speak multiple languages.

Employers also must look at alternatives to English-only rules that might have less of a discriminatory impact. For instance, if an employee reports that two coworkers made derogatory comments about a customer in Sanskrit, disciplining the two employees would be the way to deal with the issue rather than an all-out ban on foreign languages.

Direct Evidence of Discrimination

Direct evidence is where biased comments are made or actions taken specifically related to your protected status. Examples are:

Age: Referring to you as the "old man," asking when you're going to retire, saying they want a younger image.

Disability: Referring to you as the "gimp," saying they don't want your image to represent the company, making fun of your disability.

Sex: A supervisor referring to you as "sweetie" or "honey" may indicate that he looks down on women. Sexual comments about your body, other women, and sexual propositions could be sexual harassment. The same goes for comments downgrading men; both sexes can be subjected to sex discrimination.

Color: Referring to you as being too tanned or too pale.

National Origin: Saying they can't understand you when you speak fluent English with an accent, making anti-immigration comments, calling you names like "wetback" or "terrorist."

Race: Using racial terms, making generalized statements about your racial group, discussion about the evils of interracial marriage.

Indirect Evidence of Discrimination

Most supervisors aren't obvious enough to make direct comments. You can also look at others treated differently under the same circumstances. If mostly people in a different category were kept on in a layoff and people in your category are targeted, discrimination might be involved. If your category changes (you have a major birthday, or become disabled or pregnant) and are suddenly targeted for negative performance reviews and write-ups for activities other employees do, too, then you might have a discrimination claim. If people in your category are always treated differently or singled out (write-ups, denied promotions, discipline) compared to employees in a different category, you're a victim of discrimination.

Association With a Protected Person

You also can't be discriminated against due to your association with a protected person. If your child is disabled, causing the company's health insurance costs to rise; if you are married to or dating a person of a different race or national origin; if you are related to or a fiancé of a person who complained of discrimination; if you are friends with someone who has AIDS; if your parents are Muslim, you are also protected from discrimination due to that association.

Harassment

Anything that doesn't affect you in the wallet is in the category of harassment. Your employer can't make you miserable due to your protected status to try to get you to quit. You can't be called names and made fun of due to your protected status, either. However, isolated instances of name-calling may not be enough to support a claim for illegal harassment.

Special note for disability cases: Some federal circuits say that disability-based harassment is not illegal under the ADA, and some say it is illegal, so it depends where you live.

What to Do?

If it's harassment, you must report it first under the company's policy for reporting harassment and give them a chance to fix the situation. Only if they don't fix it or if the harassment continues can you file a charge of discrimination with the EEOC or your state agency.

If it's an adverse employment action like denial of a promotion, demotion, suspension without pay, or termination/layoff, you must file a charge of discrimination with the EEOC or your state agency before you can sue.

Donna's Tips

- ⊃ If you're presented with a severance agreement and think you're targeted for layoff due to any protected category, start writing down all the ways you believe you've been singled out or treated differently due to your protected category. A discrimination claim might give you leverage to negotiate a better severance package.

- ⊃ Even if the boss is your same category, that doesn't mean they can't discriminate against you. If they prefer employees in a different category than yours, it still might be discrimination.

- ⊃ Be careful when your company encourages you to apply for light duty. In order to be protected against disability discrimination, you must be able to perform all the essential duties of your job (even if you need an accommodation to do so). Once you fill out papers saying you can't do something essential, you might no longer have a covered disability under the law.

- ⊃ If you need occasional appointments for medical treatment, you might also qualify for intermittent Family and Medical Leave.

- ⊃ If your employer implements an English-only policy, the biggest question is why they did it. If they just don't like hearing Spanish all day, too bad. That's illegal. If there have been safety issues where an employee called out key instructions in Spanish and someone was hurt because they didn't understand, then the employer might have a legitimate reason for the rule.

⊃ Sometimes having a few coworkers speaking a foreign language causes problems with other employees. Morale problems may develop as people think they're being talked about behind their backs. This might also justify an English-only rule.

⊃ Election years, especially those with high-level candidates of color, can be fraught with race discrimination. Some feelings come out more publicly that you didn't know existed. Be careful when you talk politics in the office, especially with supervisors.

⊃ Write down any sexual comments, pornography, offensive e-mails, and other women who are being singled out. This may come in handy later even if you aren't being discriminated against yet. If you notice a pattern, report it even if you aren't the victim.

I Secretly Taped My Boss and Now I Want to Sue. Can I Use It in Court?

I have people come into my office all the time about sexual harassment, discrimination, or other issues who proudly pull out a DVD or tape and say "I have it all on tape." I usually jump back about 2 feet, as if the thing were a cobra (not the kind relating to insurance). That's because taping someone without their consent is a crime in my state. The tape will probably not be admissible in court, and could well land my client in jail.

I want nothing to do with recordings unless everyone whose voices appear on them consented to be recorded.

That's not true in every state. The question you should ask before you secretly record a conversation is whether your state has one-party or a two-party/all-party consent. One-party consent simply means that, if any party to the conversation agrees to be taped, it's okay. Two-party consent (also called all-party consent) requires every person who participates in the conversation to agree to be taped.

Here's how these laws apply:

Two-Party Consent: In a two-party/all-party consent state, you can't go into a disciplinary interview with a recorder hidden in your pocket to tape your employer's sexual harassment or admission that they set you up.

One-Party Consent: In a one-party consent state, as long as you are in the conversation you can tape it. You can't stand in the shadows and tape a conversation you aren't participating in to eavesdrop on what is being said. Placing a bug or hidden tape recorder in a room and leaving is always illegal unless there is a court order.

The federal law on taping, the Electronic Communications Privacy Act, has some exemptions. If a phone line is recorded for customer service, for use as a 911 line, or by court order, then the recording may be allowed. However, there are many suits over these exceptions. (This also means that many employers who tape employee conversations get it wrong). Your state law may have some exemptions too, but probably not for you as an employee.

Donna's Tips

- ☞ How do you properly tape-record a conversation in a two-party consent state? You pull out the recorder, hit the "record" button, and say: "You don't mind if I record this, do you?" If they say they don't mind, record away. If they do mind, then shut it off and put it away.

- ☞ People say the darndest things and then deny later, so the temptation to secretly record them is strong. You might want to have a witness come along instead if you're in a two-party consent state. I know it's not ideal, but it beats landing in jail.

I Was Discriminated Against Due to My Family Responsibilities. Can I Sue?

Although you may have heard about family responsibility discrimination, there is no specific law covering this category. Instead, there are a number of laws that protect people with family responsibilities from discrimination, harassment, and retaliation. Look at the following categories to see if you are covered:

Sexual Stereotyping: If your employer assumes, just because you are a woman, you are the primary caregiver and can't devote enough time to your job; because you are pregnant, you won't want to come back to work; because you are a man granted primary custody of children, you won't be able to handle your job, then you may be a victim of sexual stereotyping, which falls within illegal sexual discrimination if your employer has 15 or more employees.

Intermittent Leave: If you must care for yourself or an immediate family member with regular doctor's appointments, for instance, you are entitled up to 12 weeks a year unpaid leave. This leave can be intermittent. If the employer threatens to terminate you or does terminate you because of missing work for a serious medical condition of a family member, *and* they have at least 50 employees, *and* you've been there at least a year, you may be protected under the Family and Medical Leave Act. If you know you will need intermittent leave, notify HR in advance to assure coverage.

Pregnancy: If your employer has 15 or more employees, you can't be fired, not hired, or disciplined because you are pregnant, because of assumptions about the pregnancy and what you'll be able to do, or because of childbirth. If your doctor prescribes light duty, they don't have to give it unless they give it for any other temporarily disabled employee. Insurance must cover pregnancy, and benefits for leaves must be the same as non-pregnancy leaves.

FMLA Leave: For pregnancy or any other serious health condition (for yourself or a family member), you may be able to get up to 12 weeks of unpaid leave if your company has at least 50 employees and you've been there at least a year. While I talked about intermittent leave above, this leave can also be continuous. Twelve weeks and one day of leave means that you are no longer protected, and you don't have to be restored to the same or equivalent position. On the other hand, the employer can't use your leave to deny you an open position when you're ready to return.

Marital Status: Some states have laws protecting employees from discrimination due to being married or unmarried. The laws don't usually protect you based on being married to a particular person (such as anti-nepotism policies). However, anti-nepotism policies can't discriminate based on gender. You can't be discriminated against based on your association with someone in a protected category such as disability, race, national origin, and so forth.

Harassment: Harassment based on any of these categories is also illegal. However, you should report such harassment to HR (I suggest doing it in writing so they can't deny you reported it) and give them a chance to correct the situation. Otherwise, you may be forever barred from suing.

Adverse Action: Once you are demoted, suspended without pay, denied a position or promotion, or terminated, the laws protect you whether or not you report it to the employer first.

Donna's Tips

- If you're pregnant, find out if you're covered or will be covered under Family and Medical Leave. You might want to wait until you're showing before you tell management.

- If you have morning sickness or can only schedule doctor's appointments during work hours, you'd best tell management you're pregnant so they don't accuse you of excessive absenteeism. If you qualify for FMLA leave, apply for intermittent leave for morning sickness.

- Breastfeeding is also protected. If you must take time to pump, the employer can't discriminate.

Do I Have a Case for Genetic Information Discrimination or Harassment?

Genetic information is information about your genetic tests and the genetic tests of your family members, as well as information about any disease, disorder, or condition of your family members (family medical history).

Your employer can't use genetic information to make any employment decision about you. You can't be harassed due to your genetic information. Here's what you need to know about employers using your genetic information:

Acquiring Genetic Information: Your employer usually isn't supposed to get your genetic information. They may legally acquire genetic information if it's disclosed inadvertently (such as the supervisor overhears you talking about a family illness), as part of a voluntary health/wellness program, through FMLA certification for the illness of a family member, through publicly available information like newspapers (but they're not allowed to search for the information), and through DNA testing for law enforcement purposes.

Confidentiality: If the employer has genetic information, it must be kept in a separate file and must be kept confidential.

Donna's Tips

➲ This is a developing area of law and medical science, so it's hard to say how difficult these cases will be to win.

➲ Be careful with office chitchat about family illnesses and medical history; it's nobody's business. The company is allowed to have genetic information if they got it because you told them about it.

Can My Company Discriminate Against Me for Being Too Good-Looking, Too Ugly, or Other Aspects of My Appearance?

Usually when I see this issue come up, the standards are applied differently based on gender. Although appearance discrimination isn't illegal, sex discrimination most certainly is. When clients ask about appearance discrimination, I ask if people of the opposite sex are treated the same. Frequently, beautiful women are pigeonholed by assumptions they can't perform certain jobs, but handsome men are happily hired and promoted.

The same would apply to men. If a company hired beautiful women but didn't want handsome men in the same position (for example, receptionists, pharmaceutical reps, or waitresses), that is discrimination.

Sometimes women aren't hired or are disciplined because their clothing or makeup is not appropriate. That's not illegal. Telling female employees to tone down the clothes and high heels so they're not a distraction is probably legal as long as male employees aren't allowed to wear revealing clothes and platform shoes.

If a sexy woman isn't hired or promoted because the company assumes she'll become a sexual harassment victim, that is illegal gender stereotyping. The company has a duty to maintain a workplace that's sexual harassment–free.

I see the flipside of this question, too: People are frequently not hired due to being too ugly, too fat, or too old. Two out of three of these aren't necessarily illegal.

Too ugly. It's illegal only if it's being applied discriminatorily. I usually look at pictures of men in the company. If only women are required to be beauty queens, it's sex discrimination.

Too fat. If it's just a matter of being slightly overweight, it's probably not illegal unless only men or only women are being held to the standard. However, once the person is obese the company may cross into disability discrimination. At the very least, an obese person may be illegally regarded as disabled.

Too old. Blatantly illegal. It's still done, unfortunately. If you apply for a position and the person hired is both younger and clearly less qualified, you may have an age discrimination case.

Donna's Tips

⊃ Watch and take notes. If only women, only men, only people of a certain race/nationality are being held to certain appearance standards, it may be illegal discrimination.

⊃ If you think you're a victim of hiring discrimination, find out who got the position and their qualifications.

⊃ If you're more qualified and the person is of a different race, age, sex, national origin, color, and so on, it may be discrimination.

⊃ Don't sit on your rights. You have either 180 days or 300 days (depending on your state) to file a charge of discrimination with the EEOC. (That's a prerequisite to suing.)

Should I File With the EEOC?

The EEOC is the United States Equal Employment Opportunity Commission (*www.eeoc.gov*). If you have been the victim of discrimination, this is likely the first step you'll have to make before filing a lawsuit for discrimination. Here's what you need to know about filing with the EEOC:

Deadlines: If you work for anyone but the federal government, you must file a charge of discrimination (this is not a lawsuit) within 180 days from the date of discrimination, except where the state has its own agency that takes discrimination charges. Then the deadline is 300 days. Federal employees have 45 days to see their designated EEO counselor.

Filing Your Charge: If you're represented, your attorney can file the charge for you so you don't have to wait to meet with an investigator and go through the intake process (which can also take an hour or more). The EEOC is also doing some intakes by phone or on-line, so check with your local office.

Mediation: The EEOC will either decide to ask the parties if they want to mediate to try to resolve it, or send it straight to the investigator.

Investigation: The investigator sends a standard list of questions to the employer, along with the charge. The employer answers in what is called a position statement. You will not be given a copy of the position statement, but you still must respond to it. Some investigators call your lawyer or you, give a quick summary of a 50-page position statement on the phone, expect the attorney or you to take notes, and then give you 10 days to respond. A nice investigator will agree to summarize the position statement in a letter, and then give 10 days to respond.

Results: The EEOC is, most likely, going to issue a "Notice of Dismissal and Right to Sue." This doesn't mean you don't have a case. It means the EEOC was unable to determine whether or not you have cause for your charge because the evidence is disputed.

The other possibility is a "cause" finding. All you'll likely get out of this, besides a moral victory, is "conciliation" (an attempt to get the parties to settle). The other thing you get with a cause finding is a review by the EEOC's attorneys. The EEOC can bring a lawsuit on your behalf. This almost never happens, so don't count on it, although the EEOC has been more active in suing employers lately.

Donna's Tips

➲ You may run into an investigator who will tell you that you don't have a case. It's still your right to file, and they must take the charge if you insist. But they're right if you're trying to file for anything other than race, age, sex, national origin, genetic information, religious, color, pregnancy discrimination, or retaliation for having objected to one of these.

➲ The EEOC's mediation program is quite excellent, so I always say yes to it. Many employers and charging parties decline, which is a missed opportunity. If there's a lawsuit, you must mediate anyhow. It's free at the EEOC.

⊃ The employer will be given almost infinite extensions to re-spond to your charge, which can cause the EEOC process to drag on a year or more. Whether or not your lawyer or you are hospitalized, dying, on vacation, or kidnapped, the EEOC hates to give charging parties much of an extension to respond to a position statement. The most that is usually granted is seven to 10 days.

I Was Treated Differently Than My Coworkers. Is That Discrimination?

Favoritism is not illegal. Favoritism due to race, age, sex, religion, color, national origin, genetic information, disability, or other protected status is discrimination. Most suits for non-harassment discrimination fall within the category of "disparate treatment." This means you were treated differently than similarly situated employees under the same circumstances. You must prove:

1. **You were in a protected category.** These categories are race, age, sex, religion, national origin, pregnancy, color (meaning shade of skin color), genetic information, and disability. Some states have other categories, such as marital status or sexual orientation.

? **You were treated differently** than someone else in a different category under the same circumstances, or you were turned down for a position or promotion you were qualified for and it was given to a less qualified person.

3. **You complied with the administrative requirements** of filing with the correct agency.

Your employer must come up with a so-called legitimate reason for the action they took. This doesn't have to be a good reason, just one that is motivated by something other than discrimination.

Then, you'll have to prove that the "legitimate reason" was really pre-textual, and the real reason was discrimination. In the case of age discrimi-nation, you must prove it was the *only* reason.

➲   If your company is starting to document discipline on you, keep good records of why their accusations aren't correct.

➲   If you're keeping notes, records, or other documentation of discrimination, keep it in your purse or pocket, and take it home. Don't leave it in a desk drawer. If you are fired, the company will keep it.

➲   Don't assume your friends and coworkers will tell the truth. Most people will lie to save their jobs. Rely on your own documentation as much as possible.

I Noticed That My Employer's Testing or Other Practice Is Excluding a Protected Group of Employees. Can I Sue for That?

Some employment practices seem neutral, such as testing, height, weight, or education requirements. Even though a practice appears fair, it might have a discriminatory impact on a particular category of people. Disparate impact is why, for example, weight and height requirements were eliminated for police and fire departments. You used to see only burly guys in these jobs. Now women (and smaller men) can meet other agility requirements to prove they can do the job.

If you can show that the practice has a statistically adverse effect on a minority, your employer must prove the practice is reasonably job-related and is justified by business necessity. Then you must prove that the employer refused to implement another effective means of accomplishing the same thing that would have less of an impact.

Here's an example. The employer gives a multiple choice test that seems to be neutral, except that no women pass. The employer says: "But I must be able to test the employees' knowledge before I hire them." You then demonstrate that essay tests would accomplish the same thing, but have less of an impact on women.

➲   If you've taken a promotional exam or entry test and didn't pass, check who else failed. If you see any patterns, contact a lawyer.

➲ Disparate impact claims are dying out because the courts tend not to like them.

➲ Don't wait until people start being promoted/hired off the list. Contact a lawyer as soon as you realize there's a problem with the list. Deadlines are short, especially if you work for government.

How Do I Get a Reward for Reporting My Employer's Fraud?

You sometimes hear about whistle-blowers getting big rewards for reporting employer fraud against the government. Those cases are called *qui tam,* short for a long Latin phrase meaning "he who brings a case on behalf of our lord the King, as well as for himself." You can recover a percentage of whatever the government recovers from the fraudster if you win.

It may seem like easy money when you read about these cases, but qui tam actions are difficult to bring and prove, and even if you're right, there are still lots of ways you can lose out on being able to get your reward.

The False Claims Act is the law most qui tam cases are brought under. Many states have similar laws. It's actually a law from the Civil War, yet it's still used today.

Here's the process for bringing a qui tam case under the False Claims Act:

Attorney: You must have a lawyer. Sorry, pro se folks.

Seal: You file it under seal and it's kept on a secret docket in the court. The only people you send it to are U.S. Department of Justice, the local U.S. attorney, and the assigned judge of the district court. Sometimes you must tell the government about it before you file.

Unseal: After 60 days, the government can seek to have the seal stay in place.

Disclosure Statement: You (the relator) file a disclosure statement with the DOJ listing all the evidence you have. It's not filed in court.

Investigation: The government investigates your claims.

Investigation Ends: At the end of the investigation, the government can intervene; decline to intervene and let you pursue the case with your lawyer on behalf of the government; move to dismiss because your case conflicts with something they're already doing or some policy; or settle the case.

Intervention: If the government intervenes, they move to unseal the complaint. They usually file their own complaint that will adopt your claims and add other claims they want to bring. You'll have 120 days to serve all the named defendants with your complaint.

Suit Proceeds: After all that, the suit commences and the discovery process and depositions go forward similarly to other litigation.

First In: If you were the first to bring the fraud to the government's attention, you are probably the only one who recovers. Second to file loses.

Donna's Tips

⤳ Don't blab. If you tell your coworkers about the fraud, they might beat you to the punch. Plus, if you violate confidentiality, you're tossed out.

⤳ If you participated in the fraud, you need a criminal defense lawyer, not a qui tam lawyer. The government won't hesitate to prosecute you even if you're the hero who brings fraud to their attention. This makes them big jerks, but that doesn't mean they won't do it.

⤳ Make sure the lawyer you get is experienced in qui tam. Too many loopholes exist, too many things can go wrong, and the procedure is crazy complicated. I don't handle them, and most employment lawyers that I know don't either.

⤳ Don't forget to look at your state law process, too. Most states have similar laws.

Can My Employer Fire Me Because I Was a Domestic Violence Victim?

If you need time off for medical treatment or to seek an injunction against domestic violence, some states, city, and county ordinances protect you, but most still don't. Some states provide that employers must give you a leave of absence to deal with the effects of domestic violence; other states have laws that protect crime victims if they need time off to go to court.

If you do have to testify and your state has little or no protection for you, then you might ask the prosecutor to subpoena you. Some states prohibit retaliation against witnesses who were subpoenaed to testify.

If you are injured and your employer is large enough, you might also want to seek Family and Medical Leave.

Donna's Tips

➲ Domestic violence victims must walk a fine line because of the huge numbers of people who will look down upon you and consider you weak. Be careful who you discuss your domestic violence situation with at work.

➲ Don't assume the law protects you from retaliation. Get legal advice if you're unsure. The police may also be able to tell you whether you're protected or who can advise you (although they might give bad advice—they aren't lawyers).

➲ Don't just blow off work. Let your supervisor know you'll be out and how long.

➲ Don't delay getting the help you need. No job is worth your life or safety, or the life and safety of your loved ones.

What Can I Win If I Sue?

Damages are the monetary value of your losses that a judge or jury awards if you win a lawsuit. Damages must be reasonably foreseeable, and not speculative. Here are some of the types of damages you might see awarded in employment cases:

Lost Wages: You might see this referred to as "back pay" in discrimination, whistle-blower, and other statute-based cases. In others, it is called "lost wages." It's the difference between what you were making when you lost your job or were demoted, and what you made up to the time of the verdict. If the case is about the denial of a promotion or job, it's the difference between what you would have made and what you did make.

Future Lost Wages: An estimate of the difference you'll experience down the road. The court might allow a year, five years, or even more, depending on how long it will be before you catch up and how long it's reasonably certain to occur in the future. If you landed on your feet and got an equivalent or better job, there won't be future lost wages.

Lost Benefits: What you've already lost in the way of pension, insurance, stock, and other benefits, or even what you'll lose in the future.

Compensatory Damages: Compensation for actual losses and out-of-pocket expenses, such as medical expenses, lost wages, lost benefits, and property damage.

Emotional Distress: You don't have to go to a psychiatrist to claim emotional distress. Job loss, humiliation, and other emotional suffering can be compensated. Many employment claims don't allow emotional distress damages. Most whistle-blower statutes, Family and Medical Leave, and other statutes don't allow for emotional distress damages so you're stuck with only compensatory damages. Some state statutes allow you to recover emotional distress damages. Some states also recognize an independent tort of "intentional infliction of emotional distress."

Punitive Damages: Punitive damages are to punish reckless or intentional/malicious wrongdoing, and they are really hard to get. Although you do see some big punitive damage awards in the news, what the press rarely covers is the judge slashing them to a much smaller amount or denying them altogether.

Damage Caps: Some employment claims have a maximum amount, called a cap, that you're allowed to get if you win. It's important to know what the maximum recovery is in your case. Cases against governments usually have caps, sometimes around $100,000. In Title VII, which is where most discrimination cases fall, the damages are capped depending on how large the company is.

15–100 employees	$ 50,000
101–200 employees	$ 100,000
201–500 employees	$ 200,000
500-plus employees	$ 300,000

Donna's Tips

- ⊃ If one claim you have is capped, others might not be. For instance, state statutes on discrimination might not have the same, or any, caps on damages. You might have to pursue multiple claims in the same suit in order to be made whole.

- ⊃ Most employment cases aren't big-headline, multi-million-dollar awards. If you're lucky, you might recover lost wages and benefits.

- ⊃ Don't ever say you don't want your job back. The day you say that, you cut off your right to back pay. Even if you don't want reinstatement, it might be wise to let you lawyer keep asking for it. If it's awarded, you can always turn it down.

⊃ Don't exaggerate. Most cases don't cause you to have a nervous breakdown or get post traumatic stress disorder. If a jury thinks you're exaggerating your injuries, they'll punish you and might disbelieve your entire case.

What Is My Deadline for Bringing a Case Against My Employer?

Every claim has different time limits by which you must file suit, and some have prerequisites you must comply with before you can file. Most deadlines run from the date you were injured. This could be the date of harassment, termination, demotion, or denial of a job or raise. It could also be the first date you knew you were about to be fired, and so forth. Here are some deadlines that might affect you:

Statute Name	Agency to File With Before Suit	Deadline for Filing With Agency	Statute of Limitations for Suit
Title VII	EEOC	180 days or 300 days (depends on state)	90 days from receipt of right to sue letter
ADEA	EEOC	180 days or 300 days (depends on state)	90 days from receipt of right to sue letter
ADA	EEOC	180 days or 300 days (depends on state)	90 days from receipt of right to sue letter
42 USC §1981	None	N/A	4 years
EPA	EEOC, but not a prerequisite to filing suit	same as Title VII	2 years, 3 if violation is willful

Discrimination: The prerequisites to a discrimination lawsuit are a nightmare. Some statutes require filing with an agency; some do not. Deadlines vary, agencies vary, and messing these up can cost the plaintiff the right to bring a lawsuit. Unrepresented people frequently try to navigate this mess themselves, and many miss important deadlines or leave out crucial claims.

Here are just some of the many differences among the statutes:

Federal employees have a different set of rules, under most of the same statutes. You have 45 days to see your designated EEO counselor. There is an entire investigative process that circumvents the EEOC. Then the employee has a morass of tangled hoops to jump through.

Family and Medical Leave Act: Two years from the last event of the violations; three years for willful violations.

Sarbanes-Oxley Act: You must file a complaint with OSHA within 180 days of the date you found out about the whistle-blower discrimination, harassment, or retaliation.

National Labor Relations Act: You have six months to file a complaint with the NLRB.

Other Whistle-Blower Claims: Statutes of limitations can be as short as 30 days for some whistle-blowers protected under federal laws (e.g., environmental whistle-blowers). State whistle-blower laws vary, so know your deadlines.

Qui Tam: Within the later of six years from the date of the violation or three years after the government (or sometimes you) knows or should have known about the violation, but never longer than 10 years after the violation.

Workers' Compensation Retaliation: Varies by state. I've seen limitations periods as short as 90 days.

Assault, Battery, and Other Tort Claims: Varies by state. Generally, one to four years.

Defamation, Libel, Slander: Varies by state. Most often one to two years.

Fraud: Varies by state. Generally one to 10 years.

Breach of Contract: Varies by state. Anywhere from two to 20 years (frequently longer for written contracts than oral).

State Statutory Claims: Varies by state. It could be just about anything, depending on the claim.

Donna's Tips

➲ Don't delay if you think you have a claim. Because some claims must be pursued very quickly, delay is your enemy. Find out what potential claims you have from a lawyer and whether you have imminent deadlines.

⊃   There are very few excuses allowed for blowing a deadline, so don't do it. You'll spend more money and time litigating the issue of statute of limitations then you will on your claim. It's a huge waste to have to argue about this issue if you can avoid it.

Can I Be Fired Due to My Pregnancy or Maternity Leave?

If your employer has at least 15 employees, you can't be fired due to your pregnancy. That doesn't mean that, just because you're pregnant, you can't be fired. You can still be fired for job performance issues, job elimination, insubordination, or excessive absenteeism. Here's what you should know about pregnancy discrimination:

Maternity Leave: Even if you don't qualify for FMLA leave because your employer is too small (fewer than 50 employees), you haven't worked a year, or you work too few hours, you may still be entitled to a leave for pregnancy. Under Title VII, if you are temporarily unable to do your job because of pregnancy or childbirth, and your employer grants personal leave to anyone else, they must give you leave. So if other employees get leave to take classes, attend training, disability, or other leave, then you are also entitled to leave.

Light Duty: If temporarily disabled employees are allowed to modify their work (no heavy lifting, etc.) or are given alternate assignments, then you are also entitled to light duty. In addition, if there are job duties you never had to perform and suddenly the employer says they are "essential" and you must be able to do them or be fired, that may be pregnancy discrimination.

Fitness for Duty: You can't be singled out for a fitness for duty test just because you're pregnant. However, if the employer requires doctor's notes or information before granting sick or other leave, then they can require the same of you.

"Suddenly Stupid": If, after announcing your pregnancy, you suddenly start getting bad reviews or write-ups, or if they start asking you whether you intend to stay home and take care of the baby, you might be suffering from pregnancy discrimination.

Insurance and Benefits: Insurance must cover pregnancy-related conditions, and coverage must be the same for female employees as for spouses of male employees. You also can't be denied benefits just because you aren't married. Seniority, vacation, and other benefits must accrue during your leave the same as for any other leave the company allows.

Donna's Tips

⊃ If attitudes change suddenly once you announce your pregnancy, start keeping track. Write down comments, changed assignments or duties, and other unusual behavior. Keep it in your purse or at home so, if you are fired, they can't confiscate and "lose" it.

⊃ Do your job with extra care once you announce your pregnancy. "Pregnancy brain" isn't an excuse that will keep you from getting fired. Pregnant women are frequently the first targeted in layoffs or job elimination. Yes, it's illegal to turn you down for a new job because of your pregnancy, but do you really want to be looking for a job with a baby bump? Good luck with that.

⊃ If you are on leave, they can still do layoffs or job elimination. However, if yours is a one-person job elimination, then you might have a pregnancy discrimination claim.

⊃ If they claim they couldn't hold your job open, when you're ready to return to work check for openings in the company. They can't turn you down for a job just because you went out on maternity leave.

Can My Company Refuse to Let Me Take Religious Holidays Off or Practice My Religion at Work?

If your company has at least 15 employees, it can't discriminate against you based on your religion. They also must accommodate your religious practices, such as holidays, unless the accommodation would be an undue hardship for them. Here's what you should know about religion discrimination at work:

Sincerely Held Beliefs: You don't need to be part of an organized religion to be protected against religious discrimination. Atheists are protected. So are "moral or ethical beliefs as to what is right and wrong which are sincerely held with the strength of traditional religious views." It doesn't matter that the beliefs are illogical or even that they aren't held by many people.

For instance, a person who practices veganism for moral reasons may be protected against religious discrimination, where a person who practices veganism for health or environmental reasons may not be protected.

Religious Organizations: Religious organizations are exempt from liability for religious discrimination.

Religious Expression: Your employer can restrict your religious expression at work if it will be disruptive. For instance, they can prohibit prayers during work hours, proselytizing, and other religious activities at work as long as they prohibit them for all workers. On the other hand, they can't discriminate against you due to customer or coworker preference. For instance, if you must wear a head covering in your religion and customers complain that the company is harboring terrorists based on your appearance, the company can't fire you or demand you remove your head covering. The company may, however, have dress codes meant to appeal to customer preferences (think skimpy clothes at certain restaurants, as an example).

Dress Codes: Employers may deny requests that certain clothing be worn under limited circumstances. For instance, items that cause security concerns (such as a fez to be worn by a prison guard) may be denied. Safety concerns can be another legitimate reason to deny certain clothing (such as mandating pants rather than skirts for people working with dangerous equipment).

Time Off: If you need an accommodation, such as coming in late due to prayer sessions, not working on Saturday, or specific holidays off, the employer must grant the accommodation unless it will cause an undue hardship. Jealousy of coworkers is not an undue hardship.

Discrimination Against Others: If your religion tells you that women should be deferential to men or that certain protected groups are evil, or you hold other beliefs that require you to discriminate against others, the employer does not have to accommodate those beliefs, and you can be fired for engaging in illegal discrimination. Keep those beliefs to yourself at work.

Donna's Tips

⊃ If you need a religious accommodation, don't be shy about saying it is because of a religious practice. If you say it's for something else, then claim later it was due to religion, that can be used against you to prove it wasn't a real religious belief.

⊃ Proselytizing to others can violate their rights not to be ha-
    rassed due to religion. Be careful about pushing your beliefs
    on others.

⊃ Forcing others to participate in activities that are against their
    religious beliefs is illegal. If someone is telling you he doesn't
    want to participate in the company Halloween costume con-
    test or the Christmas party, believe him and don't push him to
    conform.

I'm Being Sexually Harassed. What Do I Do?

You're not alone if you are confused about sexual harassment. You
may suspect you're being sexually harassed but aren't sure what to do.
Maybe you're being harassed because of your gender and don't realize
you're experiencing illegal sexual harassment. Here's what you should
know about sexual harassment:

Don't Quit: Many employees quit after the first incident of sexual harassment. They're too embarrassed or scared to go back. Understandable,
but if you quit, you might lose your sexual harassment claims. The Supreme
Court says if your employer has a published sexual harassment policy, you
must report the harassment and give the employer the opportunity to fix the
situation. If you don't, you'll probably lose your sexual harassment lawsuit.

Look for the Policy: Check the handbook, posters, written policies,
union contract—anywhere there might be a sexual harassment policy.
Report it to the person designated to receive sexual harassment complaints. If they don't fix it, or if the first person designated is the harasser,
go to the next person designated.

It Doesn't Have to Be Sexual: Most people think of sexual harassment
as unwanted sexual overtures, groping, and sexual remarks. That's only
one kind of sexual harassment. If you are being harassed because you're
male or because you're female, that's sexual harassment too. Whether
you're assigned to less favorable shifts, given more difficult assignments,
placed in less lucrative territories, or being demeaned, you should report
it. I usually call this type of harassment "gender-based harassment," rather
than sexual harassment, to avoid confusion. You still must report it under
your sexual harassment policy.

Single Incident: The courts say sexual harassment must be so severe or so pervasive (meaning frequent) that it alters the terms and conditions of your employment in order to be actionable. A single comment, grope, or inappropriate e-mail probably isn't enough for a lawsuit, but it's worth reporting. Behavior that courts say isn't sexual harassment has included calling at home, asking for dates, looking down a blouse, lifting up a skirt, one or two (or even four) instances of groping, single instances of disgusting comments, rubbing, and much extreme behavior.

Investigation: The employer has a duty to investigate. They'll probably interview coworkers, the harasser, and any witnesses you designate. That also means the harasser probably will figure out you're the one who reported it. The employer might promise confidentiality, but c'mon—how many people can he or she be harassing? Scary, but the courts say you must do it anyway. Most employees, no matter how terrified, tell me they're relieved once they finally report it.

First Victim: Sexual harassment is more about power than about sex. The harasser who gets away with small violations will usually accelerate the behavior until stopped. That means you're probably not the first victim. Someone has to be the first one to come forward. If your employer turns their head at sexual harassment, they can be held strictly liable for your sexual harassment or even incur punitive damages.

Time to Quit: Okay, I know the first thing I said was "don't quit." That's generally true. But you must quit if you aren't safe, you're being driven to the brink of a nervous breakdown, or the harasser becomes physically threatening and your employer won't protect you. No case is worth getting hurt. The courts say you're only justified in quitting if no reasonable person would tolerate the behavior. That means you have an almost impossible hurdle to overcome if you sue after quitting. Only quit if you're truly risking your health, welfare, or sanity, or you have another job lined up.

Donna's Tips

➲ Even if the policy says to call or meet with someone, always put your complaint in writing. Detail every sexual comment, sexual advance, glimpse of pornography, inappropriate jokes or e-mails—anything that you've experienced or witnessed where women were treated differently than men or vice versa. Call it a "Formal Complaint of Sexual Harassment."

◌ Many employees tell me they reported a hostile environment, bullying, or harassment without saying it was because of their sex. They "didn't want to go there." Sadly, you must go there. General harassment, bullying, and a hostile work environment aren't illegal, and if you report it that way you're not protected from retaliation.

◌ You shouldn't refuse to go back just because your employer didn't fire the harasser. The law doesn't require that. Appropriate remedies may be to discipline or warn the harasser, move the harasser, transfer the victim (under some circumstances), do training, or, in extreme cases, terminate the harasser. If you didn't report it under the employer's policy before quitting, you lose your right to sue for a violation.

◌ It is the employer's duty to create a safe workplace. If you are retaliated against or continue to be harassed, report it again. If the employer allows retaliation or continued harassment, report it to the EEOC or get a lawyer.

Can I Sue for Sexual Orientation or Gender Identity Discrimination?

It's mostly legal in this country to discriminate and harass on the basis of sexual orientation and gender identity. However, more and more states, counties, and municipalities are passing laws against it. Check your state and local laws to find out if you are protected. You might be surprised, even if you think your locality is homophobic. Some conservative areas have recognized that sexual orientation discrimination has no place at work.

You have some protections nationwide, but very few:

HIV/AIDS: The ADA prohibits discrimination based on having HIV or AIDS, or being regarded as having HIV/AIDS.

Tort Claims: You are protected against assault, battery, tortious interference with your employment, defamation, and other tort claims under your state laws.

Contract: You can sue for breach of contract if you are lucky enough to have an employment contract.

Sexual Stereotyping: You may have sex discrimination claims if you are discriminated against for not fitting into stereotypical gender roles.

Federal Civil Service: The Civil Service Act of 1978 protects federal civil servants from sexual orientation discrimination.

Family and Medical Leave: If you are the caregiver for a child who becomes ill, you are covered under FMLA. You don't, however, have protection if you take leave to care for your sick partner. The Defense of Marriage Act, still in place as of the time this book was written, limits the definition of "spouse" to heterosexual married couples, even if homosexual marriage is recognized in your state. Hopefully that will change soon.

Donna's Tips

➲ I predict that, within the next decade, we'll look back on sexual orientation discrimination like we look now at pre–civil rights era race discrimination: with shame.

➲ Your company might have policies protecting you against sexual orientation discrimination and harassment. Even if you may not be legally protected against retaliation for reporting it, do utilize the company's process if it is available.

Can They Discriminate Against Me Because I'm Overweight?

If it's just a matter of being slightly overweight, it's probably not illegal unless only men or only women are being held to the standard. However, if you are obese the company may be guilty of disability discrimination. At the very least, an obese person may be illegally regarded as disabled.

As of this writing, at least one state (Michigan) has made weight discrimination illegal, and more may follow. Some municipalities have also made weight or appearance discrimination illegal.

Here's what you should know about weight discrimination:

Weight Requirements: Some weight requirements in the workplace may be illegal as having a disparate impact based on race or sex.

Major Life Activity: Once you are so overweight that it substantially affects a major life activity, then you are protected under the ADA. You may also then be eligible for reasonable accommodations for your condition.

Medical Leave: If your weight has caused a serious medical condition, you may be eligible for Family and Medical Leave.

Health Insurance: You may not qualify for certain health-related insurance discounts, but you can't be denied company health insurance due to your weight.

> ## Donna's Tips

- ⊃ Weight discrimination is more prevalent than race discrimination, so it's shocking that we, as a country, allow it. I predict that the laws will slowly change, but the overweight will be one of the last protected groups.

- ⊃ As more studies show that weight may be genetic, you may be able to look for some protection under the Genetic Information Nondiscrimination Act. Stay tuned.

Should I Blow the Whistle on My Boss? Am I a Whistle-Blower?

While most people think we have free speech in this country, there's no First Amendment in the private workplace. If you work for the government, you have limited free speech rights. Sassing your boss or complaining that she's incompetent is not protected speech.

If the company is violating the law—Medicare fraud, ripping off the government, failing to pay taxes, failing to pay wages, discriminating, polluting, and so forth, you're not automatically a whistle-blower. However, if you report or refuse to participate in the illegal activity, there are a host of whistle-blower laws that may protect you. Find out which law protects you, and make sure you complain in a way that's protected. Some laws require you complain in writing to a supervisor. Some say you must report the company to a government agency. Some only require that you object to or refuse to participate in the illegal activity. If you get it wrong, you aren't protected from retaliation.

These are just some examples of activities that might be protected:

Objection to Illegal Activity: Under many whistle-blower laws, but not all, your objection must be in writing. But an objection to a breach of the employer's policies, or to an ethical violation, is generally not whistle-blowing. Your long letter venting about every way the workplace is unprofessional may be satisfying, but it can get you fired.

The objection likely must be to an activity, policy, or practice of the employer. If you object to a coworker stealing from the company, it's probably not protected, but objecting to failure to pay overtime, discrimination based on a protected category (race, age, sex, religion, national origin, marital status, disability, color, and, in a few states and localities, sexual orientation), safety violations governed by OSHA, and violation of statutes, government regulations is.

Even if the objection doesn't need to be written, I suggest you put it in writing so the employer can't deny you made the objection later.

Refusal to Participate in Illegal Activity: If the employer asks you to do something actually illegal, whistle-blower laws applying to your industry may say you can refuse and you are protected. I still suggest you put your refusal in writing.

Disclosing Illegal Policies, Activities, or Practices: You may be protected if you have brought the activity, policy, or practice to the attention of a supervisor or the employer and have given the employer a reasonable opportunity to correct the activity, policy, or practice (for example, you made a formal written complaint of sex discrimination). The formal complaint says that if the situation is not promptly resolved, you intend to file a charge of discrimination with the EEOC. Then you may be protected from retaliation.

Testifying in an Investigation, Hearing, or Inquiry by a Government Agency: If you give information to the police, unemployment, the EEOC, OSHA, a legislative body, or other entity actually doing an investigation of an illegal practice, you may be a protected whistle-blower.

The Whistle-Blower Laws

The remedies, requirements, and administrative hoops are the subject of entire treatises, so I'll draw your attention to some of the major whistle-blower laws. The federal whistle-blower laws are:

The OSHA-enforced laws govern protection of workers against retaliation for complaining to employers, unions or the Occupational Safety and Health Administration (OSHA), or other government agencies about unsafe or unhealthful conditions in the workplace, the environment, some public safety hazards, and some securities fraud violations. The OSHA-enforced laws include Occupational Safety and Health Act, Surface Transportation Assistance Act, Asbestos Hazard Emergency Response Act, International Safety Container Act, Energy Reorganization Act of 1974, Clean Air Act, Safe Drinking Water Act, Federal Water Pollution Control Act, Toxic Substances Control Act, Solid Waste Disposal Act,

Comprehensive Environmental Response, Compensation, and Liability Act, Wendell H. Ford Aviation Investment and Reform Act, Sarbanes-Oxley Act, Pipeline Safety Improvement Act, Federal Railroad Safety Act, National Transit Systems Security Act, Consumer Product Safety Improvement Act, and Affordable Care Act.

Sarbanes-Oxley is the most famous OSHA-enforced whistle-blower law. It protects employees of publicly traded corporations from retaliation for reporting violations of SEC rules and federal laws regarding fraud against shareholders.

The Whistleblower Protection Act protects Federal employee whistle-blowers.

The Military Whistleblower Protection Act protects whistle-blowers in the U.S. military.

The False Claims Act (FCA) enables a private citizen to file a lawsuit in on behalf of the U.S. government for fraud by contractors and other businesses that use federal funds. Qui tam prohibits an employer from retaliating against an employee for attempting to report fraud against Medicare, Medicaid, the FDA, GSA, HUD, USDA, the U.S. Postal Service, NIH, and the military, but not the IRS.

State Whistle-Blower Laws

Some states have whistle-blower protection laws for most employees, government or private, and others offer whistle-blower protection to government, but not private employees. Some states have no whistle-blower protections.

Other Retaliation

Here are some examples of other types of complaints where the law protects you from retaliation:

Discrimination: If you are the victim of discrimination or harassment based upon your race, age, sex, religion, national origin, color, disability, genetic information, or association with a person in one of these categories or another category that's protected in your state/county/city (for example, marital status or sexual orientation), then you may be protected if you follow your employer's published discrimination/harassment policy and report it or if you file with the EEOC.

Wage/Overtime Violations: If you're terminated for objecting to failure to pay wages owed or failure to pay overtime, you may be protected from retaliation under the Fair Labor Standards Act or your state's wage/hour laws.

Collective Action to Improve Working Conditions: The National Labor Relations Act protects employees from being retaliated against if they get together to try to improve the terms and conditions of their employment.

Donna's Tips

- ⊃ Put your complaint in writing even if the employer's policy says to have a meeting. You can present the written document at the meeting. That way you have proof you complained about something protected. Otherwise, HR will almost always say you complained about general harassment or unfair treatment, which isn't protected.

- ⊃ If you complain, keep it professional and to the point. Avoid complaining about personality conflicts or incompetence. Stick to the facts that prove what's happening is illegal.

- ⊃ HR is entitled to investigate your complaint. The person you're complaining about, and your witnesses and other coworkers will probably find out about it.

- ⊃ If you are retaliated against for reporting something illegal, put your complaint of retaliation in writing. If the retaliation doesn't stop, or if you get fired, disciplined, or demoted, or a pay cut as a result, contact an employment attorney or the government agency that handles the law you reported violations under.

- ⊃ If, after you complain, the situation is not fixed, contact an employment attorney for advice.

- ⊃ They don't have to fire anyone or take any specific action, so don't threaten to quit if they don't fire the perpetrator.

- ⊃ If you're complaining about a boss or coworker embezzling, stealing, or doing something *to* the company, as opposed to on behalf of the company, you're probably not protected from retaliation. Lots of people get fired for reporting someone ripping off the company. Silly, yes, but there you have it. Killing the messenger is alive and well.

Do I Have a Case Under Sarbanes-Oxley?

Sarbanes-Oxley (SOX) is the most well-known of the whistle-blower laws. However, it does not apply to most whistle-blower cases. Here's what you should know about SOX:

Retaliation: It is illegal for certain publicly traded companies, nationally recognized statistical rating organizations, and any officers, employees, contractors, subcontractors, and agents of those companies to retaliate against you if you blow the whistle on securities fraud and other misrepresentations to shareholders and prospective shareholders.

Protected Activity: Providing information, causing information to be provided, or assisting in a government investigation by a government agency, law enforcement agency, member of Congress, or congressional committee, or in an internal company investigation (by a supervisor or person with authority to investigate), relating to mail fraud, wire fraud, bank fraud, securities fraud, SEC rules/regulations violations, or shareholder fraud is protected. So is assisting in or bringing a legal proceeding regarding any of this type of legal violation.

Criminal Penalties: In addition to civil penalties, anyone who retaliates against a SOX whistle-blower could land 10 years in prison.

Types of Prohibited Retaliation: The employer cannot retaliate by firing or laying off, blacklisting, demoting, denying overtime, suspending, denying promotion, disciplining, denying benefits, failing to hire or rehire, intimidating, threatening, harassing, reassigning, or reducing pay/hours.

Procedure: If you are a victim of SOX whistle-blower retaliation, you must file a complaint with OSHA first, within 180 days from the date of the violation or the date you become aware of the violation. If there is no final agency decision within 180 days after you file, you can sue in federal court.

Donna's Tips

⊃   The truth is that most SOX whistle-blower claims are dismissed at the administrative agency level. You have an uphill battle bringing SOX claims.

⊃   If you participated in the illegal activity at all, you might become the target of a criminal prosecution. Some whistleblowers who uncovered huge scandals have landed in prison. Be very, very careful.

I Was Wrongfully Terminated. Can I Sue?

You want to sue for wrongful termination. If you live in Montana, your employer would need to have cause to fire you. Every other state is at-will, meaning your employer can fire you for any reason or no reason at all.

That doesn't mean there are no protections for employees. Ask yourself the following questions to see if you are covered:

Did my supervisors make any comments indicating bias? If your supervisor made racist or sexist jokes, said they thought you were too old or that your disability made you unable to do the job, required you to work on religious holidays, or made other comments that indicate bias, you may have direct evidence of discrimination.

Was I treated differently than others in the same situation? If you don't have direct evidence of discrimination, were you treated differently than those of a different race, sex, religion, national origin, age, or other protected status under the same circumstances? Think of people who are of a different race, age, sex, and so forth, and were treated differently from you. Find out if there are people who have also been the victims of similar discrimination.

Why was I really fired? Most employees have a pretty good idea why they were fired. If you made a workers' compensation claim and were fired a week later, that's a good indication you were fired in retaliation for making the claim. If you reported your company's shareholder fraud, then you're fired, you may have a whistle-blower claim.

Is my employer saying something false about me? If potential employers say you are going to be hired if your references check out, and then the job is mysteriously filled when you call back, your employer may be giving false or damaging information about you. There are professional reference-checking companies that will call for you and see what an employer is saying about you. If you can prove it's false, you may be able to sue for defamation.

Am I in some protected category? If you were fired after you took some protected action, you may be able to sue for retaliation. Think about whether you recently made a workers' compensation claim, performed jury duty, served in the military, took Family and Medical Leave, served as a witness in a lawsuit, provided testimony or evidence to the EEOC, refused to participate in illegal activity, reported illegal activity, or engaged in protected free speech.

Read this book. Even if you think you aren't protected, you might find that you are.

Donna's Tips

○ If you believe something illegal has happened, contact an attorney in your state to discuss the possibility of a case.

○ Even if nothing illegal happened, many employers will discuss a severance agreement. Sometimes an amicable transition is the best way for both employer and employee to move on in a positive direction.

○ If you are offered a severance package, have an attorney review it prior to signing. Many employment attorneys will work to negotiate a better package for you.

What's it Like to Be in a Lawsuit?

I'm always surprised by people who say: "Do we have to try to negotiate with them first? Can't I just sue?" Those people almost certainly have never been in a lawsuit before. The truth is that, in more than 25 years of law practice, I've never had one single client say, at the end of a lawsuit, win or lose, "I'm really glad I did that."

Lawsuits are expensive, emotionally draining, long, drawn-out, and frustrating, and they take away from your ability to hold down a job. Here's why:

Slow-Moving Courts: One thing you hardly hear about, unless you're a lawyer, is that a huge side effect of the recession was that courts got bogged down with foreclosures. That's bad news for anyone trying to move a suit along. Whereas I used to say lawsuits take about a year, where I live it's more like two or three years. When it used to take a month to get a 30-minute to one-hour hearing, it now takes six months. Short hearings used to take a week, and now take about three weeks to get set.

Constant Attacks: If you think presidential candidates are the most attacked people on Earth, try filing a lawsuit. You will hear every piece of dirt the company can drag up on you. They'll dig up past employers, coworkers you thought were your friends—anyone who will say anything nasty about you. Forget about those stellar reviews. You'll hear you were the worst employee on the planet.

Depositions: You'll have to sit for a deposition where the attorney on the other side asks you lots of nasty questions. Not fun. And you must miss a day of work for it.

Missed Work: You'll not only miss work for your deposition. You may want to sit in on some or all of the depositions taken of key witnesses. You may also want to attend important hearings. And of course you must attend the trial. Can you say excessive absenteeism? And guess how pleased your new employer will be to hear about you suing your former employer?

Expenses: Court reporter fees are huge. Add in mediator fees, filing fees, process server fees, expert witness fees, copies, couriers, and so on, and that money starts draining pretty fast.

Risk: You not only risk losing the case, but also paying the other side's attorney's fees and costs if you lose in many cases.

Donna's Tips

- ⊃ Do not take filing a lawsuit lightly. You must be in it for the long haul. It will take up a good chunk of your life for a long time.

- ⊃ It's not like on TV in any way, shape, or form. Don't get your legal advice from TV shows.

What Should I Expect If I Contact a Lawyer?

Before you even get to a lawyer's office, you may be pre-screened. Some attorneys allow staff to speak with you to make sure your issue is in their area of practice before setting the appointment; some have you meet with paralegals or other staff and fill out a questionnaire before being allowed to meet with the attorney; some (like me) prescreen by asking questions on the phone or by e-mail.

Most attorneys have a questionnaire to fill in with basic information. Some people tell me they don't want to fill it in, or that it doesn't apply.

You must fill out the lawyer's questionnaire to the best of your ability. You wouldn't go into a doctor's office and say you don't need to fill out your forms, would you? Lawyers need this information to help you. If you can't be bothered to spend a little time explaining why you're there and give them information they need, why should they bother with your case? Many of us are very busy and can pick and choose our clients.

Once the intake form is completed, the lawyer meets with you to ask questions to decide whether or not there's a case. If you have any documents, such as unemployment determinations, reviews, disciplines, a termination letter, a contract, or other information that the lawyer might need to decide whether or not you have a case, bring it! I hate it when I ask whether the client has something and the answer is "Oh yeah. At home." How can we help you if you don't bring what we need?

If the lawyer decides to take your case, you will be expected to sign a retainer agreement that reflects the fee arrangement, any costs to be incurred, the extent of the relationship, and anything else that must be addressed at the beginning.

Legal Fees

Contingency: If you watch lots of personal injury commercials, you probably think all lawyers work this way. They don't. A contingency fee is just what it sounds like: The contingency is getting a result (settlement, severance, and so forth). The fee is paid only if the attorney succeeds, and is based on a percentage of the recovery. The maximum the Bar usually allows is 40 percent, although higher percentages can be done with court approval. I've never heard of that actually happening, but I assume it does from time to time. Few employment cases are done on a straight contingency basis, at least where I live. Generally, the only thing I do on a straight contingency is severance negotiation. Even if they do your case on a straight contingency, most attorneys require their clients to pay for costs as they go along.

Flat Fees: These are set fees for a particular service. You see them commonly for EEOC representation, letter writing, drafting contracts, forms—virtually anything that the lawyer can predict how much time will be involved.

Hourly Rates: These are just what they sound like. Rates depend on the attorney's reputation and experience. If you've been sued by your former employer, such as for a non-compete, you'll pay hourly. Many firms get a retainer up front for some portion of the case, ranging usually between $1,000 and $15,000, and then bill after that retainer is exhausted. If you sue and end up with a counterclaim against you, the lawyer may handle that on an hourly basis.

Hourly/Contingency Hybrid: This is a combination. The hourly is reduced, ranging from, say, $50 to $150, and the contingency is reduced to anywhere between 10 percent and 33.33 percent.

Partial Contingency: You pay a flat fee, usually nonrefundable, up front. The rest is based on a contingency, ranging from 20 percent to 33.33 percent.

Donna's Tips

⊃ Don't waste your time and the attorney's by withholding vital information just so you can get the appointment. If you already have a lawsuit pending, have another lawyer, were fired years ago, or got a demand letter from your former employer, for heaven's sake, tell the attorney that up front.

⊃ Don't lie to your lawyer. She must know the truth from you. Your lawyer can't tell anyone what you say without your permission. If you lie, she can't help you. If you lie and get caught later, your case will be dismissed and the lawyer will probably withdraw.

⊃ Be prepared for your meeting. Organize your notes and evidence. If you don't care about your case, what busy lawyer will want to help you?

⊃ Don't be nasty to the lawyer or his staff. Most lawyers don't take every case that walks in the door. Consider the interview with the lawyer like a job interview. Impress him that you have a case, will make a good and reliable witness, and will cooperate with him.

What Is Mediation and Should I Agree to Participate in It?

You may not have a choice on whether or not to mediate. If you're in a lawsuit, you will almost certainly be ordered to mediate. If you have filed with the EEOC, they offer free mediation. Agree to it. It's a great way to try to settle your case without the hassle of going through a lawsuit. Here's what you need to know about mediation:

The Mediator: Mediators are trained in tactics to help the parties reach a consensus. They are neutral third parties who have no stake in the outcome of your case. Mediators must disclose any conflicts, prior dealings with either side or the attorney, or other potential matters that could affect their impartiality. The parties can object to any mediator and will usually be asked to agree on one. Sometimes the court or agency will appoint one, subject to objection.

Openings: Mediation usually starts with a session where everyone is present. The attorneys, a party representative if it's a corporation, the party if it's an individual, and the insurance adjuster (if there's insurance), are present, or sometimes on the phone. The mediator explains the process, and gives each side time to explain their side of the dispute and what efforts have been made to settle. Some lawyers tell me that, in their states, mediations rarely start with the parties together. Openings depend on mediator preference and local practice.

Caucus: Most mediations break into "caucuses," where the mediator meets with each side to discuss the upsides and downsides of the case and settlement offers to be relayed. What is discussed in caucus is confidential unless you give the mediator permission to relay it to the other side.

The mediator then goes back and forth between the parties, relaying information and offers, asking questions, making sure both sides understand the risks of going to trial, and trying to reach a settlement. Mediators can't give legal advice or put pressure on any side, and they can't prefer one side over the other.

Settlement: Most cases settle at mediation. If mediation is successful, the parties walk out with a signed settlement agreement. If unsuccessful, impasse is declared and the case goes on to the next step.

Donna's Tips

- ⊃ Bring something to do. Caucuses with employers can take a long, long time. Bring a book, bills to pay, your computer, video games—anything that keeps you busy and your mind on other things during long breaks.

⊃   Keep an open mind. Listen to the mediator and your lawyer if you have one. If you come in with a specific settlement number in mind and are inflexible, you will be less likely to settle.

⊃   The trend, at least in my locality, seems to be for longer and longer mediations. My personal belief is that you will get careless and impatient the longer the mediation lasts. I prefer to end mediation after three to four hours. If the parties are making progress and it needs to go longer, a second session can be scheduled.

Crisis Scenarios on Having a Case Against Your Employer

Scenario 1

Your boss is picking on you. He gives you most of the workload and criticism. Your coworkers aren't treated this way. You think it's because he believes you're making too much money. Do you:

❑ a. Complain to HR about his bullying?

❑ b. Tell him you don't have to do more than your fair share of work, then refuse to take the next assignment he piles on?

❑ c. Tough it out? He's a bully. It might be time to look for a new job.

If you answered a:
That's fine if your company has an anti-bullying policy. Still, you have put yourself at risk because you aren't legally protected from retaliation. Bullying isn't illegal.

If you answered b:
You are probably fired. At the very least, you are about to be written up for insubordination.

If you answered c:
You're right. He's a jerk. Get the heck out of there.

Scenario 2

Same as scenario 1, except you think the reason he's picking on you is you're Arabic. All your coworkers and your boss are Hispanic. Do you:

❑ a. Complain to HR about national origin harassment?

❑ b. Next time he treats you differently than coworkers, tell him you're going to file with the EEOC?

❑ c. Quit, then sue the bastard?

If you answered a:

You're playing it smart. Make sure you say it's a complaint about national origin harassment, and put it in writing. If they retaliate, then you can go to the EEOC or talk to an employment lawyer.

If you answered b:

That's an okay move. But he's an SOB, so he'll deny you ever said it. Although you're technically legally protected against retaliation, you'd be better off going to HR or whoever your employer's harassment policy says to report it to.

If you answered c:

You jumped the gun. You must follow their published harassment policy and report it first. Give them a chance to resolve the situation. Otherwise, you might lose your right to sue.

Scenario 3

Your boss asks you when you're going to retire. When she places an ad for a new employee at your level, she says she's looking for someone with a younger image. Shortly after she hires a 21-year-old with little experience, your job is eliminated. Do you:

❑ a. Complain to HR about age discrimination?

❑ b. Put in for retirement?

❑ c. File with the EEOC or contact a lawyer about pursuing an age discrimination claim?

If you answered a:

This isn't a bad idea, but you don't have to do it before you file your charge of discrimination with the EEOC. Because you're fired, you don't have to jump through the hoop of reporting it under the company's harassment policy.

If you answered b:

If you qualify, go for it. If you opt for early retirement, you may lose increased benefits. You might talk to a lawyer. Maybe they can negotiate a severance package that gets you to full retirement if you're close.

If you answered c:

Even if you put in for retirement, you should still do this. Unless you've signed a severance package releasing all your claims, you may well have a discrimination case.

Scenario 4

You've reported sexual harassment to human resources. You get a call from the VP of human resources. The company attorney and he want to meet with you to interview you about your complaint. Do you:

❏ a. Refuse to meet? You have the right to remain silent.

❏ b. Refuse to meet unless you have your lawyer present?

❏ c. Panic? "I need more time. Can we meet next month?"

❏ d. Say: "Thank you. Let me know when and where."? Work on gathering evidence to take with you.

If you answered a:

You've been watching too many TV shows. The right to remain silent applies to criminal investigations by the police, not to an investigation by HR. If you refuse to meet, they will assume you are lying. It won't be much of an investigation, and failing to cooperate with the investigation might be a defense for the company if you sue later.

If you answered b:

They probably won't let you have a lawyer present at an internal company meeting. If you ask politely whether your lawyer may attend, they may agree but don't have to. If you are a member of a union, you may have the right to be accompanied by a union representative. If you aren't allowed to have a lawyer present, take good notes about the questions asked and your answers so you can show your lawyer later. If you have an attorney, let her know about the meeting. If you're represented, the company attorney can't meet with you without your lawyer's permission, but HR can.

If you answered c:

Some employees refuse or delay this meeting. Being called into a meeting like this is a good sign. Your employer is doing what they're supposed to do, which is conduct a reasonable investigation. (Either that or you're being set up to be fired, but let's stay optimistic.) By delaying the meeting, you may force them to investigate without you. It's better to give your side first so they know what to ask other witnesses and what evidence to gather.

If you answered d:

Good for you! Now get ready. Make notes to take with you. If you haven't already, put together a written "Formal Complaint of Sexual Harassment." If you have written proof (e-mails, memos, photos, recordings—not illegal tape recordings of conversations, though, or other documents), gather them to bring to the meeting.

Scenario 5

Your boss is sexually harassing you. You don't want it to be a he said/she said situation, but he's too smart. Nobody has witnessed what he's saying. Do you:

- ❑ a. Hide a tape recorder? Record his nasty sexual overtures and take the tape to HR as proof.
- ❑ b. Take good notes of his comments? List times, dates, and places. When you have several good ones, write up a Formal Complaint of Sexual Harassment and send it to HR.
- ❑ c. Dial your cell phone to call your home phone? Let the answering machine record what he's saying.

If you answered a:

If you live in a state where this is legal, do it. However, if you get it wrong and your state requires all parties to consent to being recorded, you may go directly to jail.

If you answered b:

This is your only option if you live in a state with all-party consent. The specific dates and times will help your credibility when you go to HR. Don't give them your only copy or your original. Type your notes or copy them to give.

If you answered c:

Sorry, but nobody's buying this was an accident. See answer a.

Scenario 6

You have diabetes. Your employer tells you there will be no breaks during your busy season, which lasts for two months. You must eat at least every four hours to keep your blood sugar level steady. Do you:

- ❑ a. Sneak a snack whenever you can? Slip into the bathroom or break room and eat when nobody is looking.
- ❑ b. Put in a written request for reasonable accommodation for your disability, asking for short snack breaks every four hours?
- ❑ c. Tough it out? You need your job.

If you answered a:

If your company has fewer than 15 employees, this might be what you should do. You have no legal protection under ADA. However, with a bigger employer this is risky. If caught, you could be fired for insubordination.

If you answered b:

Assuming your employer has 15 or more employees, this is your best move. They can't deny the accommodation unless they can show undue hardship. They can't fire you for requesting an accommodation. (Well, they can, but it would be illegal retaliation.)

If you answered c:

You'll end up in the hospital if you do this, or worse. Don't risk your health for a job.

Scenario 7

Your son needs surgery. You've been working for nine months, full-time. Do you:

- ❑ a. Put in for Family and Medical Leave?
- ❑ b. Put in for a vacation to cover the time of his surgery?
- ❑ c. Call in sick when he goes in for the procedure?

If you answered a:

It will be denied. You must work at least a year to be covered, and your employer must have at least 50 employees within 75 miles of your work location.

If you answered b:

This is probably your best bet. Of course, if your vacation is suddenly rescinded due to a work emergency, you have trouble. With little legal protection, you must handle this carefully. You might want to arrange a backup person to be with him just in case you must work.

If you answered c:

You are probably going to be fired. You left them in the lurch, and you weren't sick.

Scenario 8

Your son is deaf and he has surgery to install a cochlear implant. You take your vacation because your employer only has 20 employees. A few weeks later, your boss starts making comments about how they must be careful about health insurance costs. You're fired a week later in a one-person layoff. Do you:

❑ a. Apply for unemployment? It's terrible, but you weren't protected by any law.

❑ b. Talk to an employment lawyer about a possible Family and Medical Leave Act violation?

❑ c. Talk to the EEOC or an employment lawyer about a possible disability discrimination claim?

If you answered a:

You should apply for unemployment, but you do have legal protection under the Americans with Disabilities Act.

If you answered b:

Sorry. You aren't protected by FMLA because the employer is too small. However, if you go to an employment lawyer, he might be able to advise you that you have a potential ADA claim.

If you answered c:

Smart! You figured out that you were probably fired due to your association with a person with a disability—namely, your son. That's illegal.

Scenario 9

You take time off for your mother's funeral. Your boss is very sympathetic until she finds out your mother died of a condition that is genetic. She asks you if you inherited the gene. She starts muttering about insurance costs and absenteeism. You get write-ups and bad reviews despite the fact that you had all excellent reviews in previous years. Do you:

❑ a. Complain to HR about bullying?

❑ b. File with the EEOC for disability discrimination?

❑ c. Complain to HR about genetic information discrimination?

If you answered a:

You can do that, but you aren't protected against retaliation. Bullying isn't illegal.

If you answered b:

You probably jumped the gun, because you didn't complain through the company's harassment policy. You may be protected under ADA if your supervisor now regards you as disabled.

If you answered c:

This is probably your best bet, although you might also want to add that she regards you as disabled. It's illegal to discriminate against you based on your genetic information.

Scenario 10

You take pride in your looks. Other women sometimes take an instant dislike to you because you are just too pretty. Your new boss is one of them. She obviously considers you a threat. She tells you to tone down your clothing. She says you dress too sexy and don't look professional. Do you:

❑ a. Tell her you can wear whatever you want? Continue dressing to impress.

❑ b. Go to HR and complain about sexual harassment?

❑ c. Tone it down? Try to dress more like other people in the office.

If you answered a:

You are probably on your way out. You're being insubordinate.

If you answered b:

Sorry, but unless she lets men wear revealing clothes and not women, this isn't sex discrimination or sexual harassment. Employers can discriminate based on your appearance. They are allowed to hate you because you're beautiful.

If you answered c:

Good move. If your supervisor thinks you are too distracting or dressing unprofessionally, she might be right. It's best to dress similarly to others in the office, especially like those in management.

Scenario 11

Your company orders you to do things you know are illegal. Do you:

❏ a. Put in writing that you object to and refuse to participate in the illegal activities?

❏ b. Go along quietly, then report them to the appropriate government agency?

❏ c. Tell them unless they pay you to stay quiet you'll blow the whistle?

If you answered a:

This may make you a protected whistle-blower under many whistle-blower statutes. But be sure of the statute that applies and what you must do to be protected. Definitely don't do anything that could get you arrested.

If you answered b:

If you are participating in illegal activity, then you might be arrested even if you blow the whistle. It's best to report them only if you aren't a participant.

If you answered c:

You've now officially participated in blackmail. If they decide to report you to the police, you're going to jail.

Scenario 12

You announce you're pregnant. Suddenly, you're excluded from meetings. You get written up for things everyone else does, too. You get your first bad review ever. When the company has a mass layoff, you're the only person at your level selected, although you have more experience and qualifications than three coworkers who are still there. They present you with a severance agreement. Do you:

❏ a. Sign it and take the money? You can't afford not to now that you're pregnant.

❑ b. Sign, then file a charge of discrimination with the EEOC for pregnancy discrimination?

❑ c. Have a lawyer review the agreement to see if there is leverage to negotiate a better package?

If you answered a:

You've released all pregnancy discrimination claims, and any other claims you might have. You might have also signed a non-compete agreement or other limitation on your ability to work. Be careful what you sign.

If you answered b:

You absolutely can do this, but you probably gave up your right to recover any money even if the EEOC were to miraculously decide to sue on your behalf (ha!). You likely gave up your right to sue for money.

If you answered c:

You made the right decision. It's possible the package is a good one. But maybe the pregnancy discrimination claim will give you some leverage to negotiate. If the employer won't negotiate, you can either sign, or walk away and pursue your legal claims. At least you'll know what your options are and what you're signing.

Scenario 13

Your religion requires you not to work on a specific day. You tell your boss a month in advance and he shrugs. The day before your religious holiday, he says you must work the following day or be fired. Do you:

❑ a. Contact HR to ask that your religious accommodation be granted?

❑ b. Call in sick the following day?

❑ c. Tell your boss he can't make you work on a religious holiday? Take the holiday anyhow.

If you answered a:

You're playing it smart. Human resources may be able to intervene to help. The company must grant a religious accommodation unless it can show an undue hardship.

If you answered b:

You're probably fired. Your boss knows you deliberately violated a direct order.

If you answered c:

Though you may get away with this, you might have to protest your termination to HR. You might end up fired and having to file with the EEOC if the company won't relent. It's usually best to get a religious accommodation approved in writing well in advance.

Scenario 14

Your company announces an upcoming golf tournament. Your male co-workers get invitations. When you question why you weren't invited, your boss says: "You can participate in women's favorite sport: shopping." You're regularly excluded from important meetings. Your quotas are always higher than your male colleagues. Do you:

❑ a. Insist you be allowed to attend the golf tournament? Crash if they say no.

❑ b. File with the EEOC for sex discrimination?

❑ c. File a formal written complaint of gender-based harassment with HR?

If you answered a:

That's one way to go, but you won't make any friends. You might not be protected from retaliation if you take this approach because you haven't engaged in any legally protected activity.

If you answered b:

You jumped the gun. You must file under the company's published sexual harassment policy and give them a chance to address the situation first before you take legal action.

If you answered c:

This is what the courts require you to do if you are harassed due to your gender. Use the company's sexual harassment policy and give them a chance to fix the situation. If it continues, or if they retaliate, talk to an employment attorney or the EEOC.

7 The End:

Layoffs, Terminations, References, Severance

What Are My Rights If I've Been Fired?

Many employees believe their termination must be done a particular way. There's no specific requirement in most states for firing you. Here's what you need to know about your rights if you're fired:

Reasons for Termination: Unless you have a contract saying you can only be fired for cause, the employer doesn't have to give any reason for firing you under federal law. Some state unemployment statutes require the employer to give you general reasons (layoff, discharge, and so forth) by a deadline so you can file for unemployment.

Written Termination Papers: The company doesn't have to give you a letter or written notice of termination under federal law. Some state laws and contracts require the employer give you a termination notice.

Reference: The company doesn't have to give you a reference or even return the calls of a prospective employer. However, refusal to give references might be evidence of retaliation if you raised issues of discrimination or are a protected whistle-blower.

Non-Compete: If you're fired for no reason, it's still possible your former employer could enforce a non-compete agreement.

Signing Termination Papers: There's nothing requiring you to sign anything about your firing. If your employer gives you something to sign, if you aren't getting anything for it (severance, unemployment, and so on), take a pass. If you decide to sign, understand what you're giving away in exchange.

Donna's Tips

- ⊃ Don't burn bridges. If you're fired, it's tempting to blast your supervisor and everyone involved. Most industries are small; that former supervisor or HR person may well end up at your new employer.

- ⊃ Just because you've been fired doesn't mean you can't go back. Unless you're listed as ineligible for rehire, many employees leave for a year or more and end up rehired.

- ⊃ If you can get written reference letters from friendly supervisors/managers, do so. That way they can't say you were a poor performer later.

What Should I Say in My Exit Interview? Should I Go?

Some companies demand you do an exit interview after you've been fired. They can't make you do this. I'd suggest not doing it unless they offer to pay you for your time.

The purpose of an exit interview is for the company to cover itself in case you later claim discrimination or something illegal. If you go, make any allegations of discrimination, unpaid wages, safety violations, illegal harassment, whistle-blower retaliation, and so forth in writing while you're there. If you're too shaken to remember, follow up the interview in writing with the allegations.

Avoid the temptation to blast your supervisor, or complain about incompetence, mismanagement, or other general complaints. Remember: These are the folks who will be giving references to potential employers.

Donna's Tips

- ⊃ Find out the purpose of the interview and who will be attending before you go.

- ⊃ You probably won't be allowed to bring your lawyer.

⊃ If you don't see the upside, don't go.

⊃ You may be offered severance or be asked to sign documents. Don't sign anything until you fully understand it.

What Is this COBRA Paperwork I Just Got?

COBRA, the Consolidated Omnibus Budget Reconciliation Act, lets workers and their families who lose their insurance pay to continue coverage on their own through their former employers. Here's what you need to know about your COBRA coverage:

Covered Employers: Employers with 20 or more employees probably must provide COBRA continuation. If they've had 20 or more employees 50 percent or more of the past year, you're protected. Part-time employees count as part of an employee. Say the company has 20 half-day employees; they count as 10 employees. Some states have "mini-COBRA" statutes that cover smaller employers. The federal government has a program similar to COBRA for federal employees.

Covered Individuals: Anyone who was covered under a group health insurance plan the day before what's called a "qualifying event" is allowed to buy continued coverage. That includes the employee, spouse, children, former spouse, and other dependents.

When Covered: A qualifying event triggering COBRA coverage is anything that causes you to lose coverage: being fired, quitting, being cut to part-time, or a layoff. For spouses or dependents, divorce, disability/death of the covered employee, or the covered employee becoming qualified for Medicare also triggers COBRA.

When Do You Lose COBRA Rights?: Gross misconduct of the former employee can cost the entire family the right to COBRA. If the employer drops coverage or goes bankrupt, there is generally no COBRA continuation, because there is no insurance unless the company gets a new plan.

How Long?: COBRA lasts generally up to 18 months, but if you become disabled you can apply for more. Also, Congress periodically extends COBRA benefits or provides subsidies in the event of a financial crisis, so understand your rights.

What Happens to Coverage While You're Waiting for COBRA to Kick In: Your insurance coverage may get cut off the very day you are terminated. Don't be surprised if you can't fill a prescription or must pay out of pocket for a doctor's appointment. Don't worry too much. The insurance goes back into effect retroactively once you pay COBRA premiums.

How Long Will it Take to Get Coverage Again?: The employer must tell the plan administrator you had a qualifying event within 30 days. The administrator must send you a notice explaining your rights within 14 days after the administrator finds out from the employer. Each beneficiary gets a notice and has the right to elect coverage. Then you'll have 60 days to elect COBRA coverage.

Donna's Tips

➲ No doubt about it: COBRA coverage is crazy expensive. You end up paying 100 percent of what the employer was paying, plus a 2-percent administrative fee. Still, if a family member or you need surgery or have an accident, there's no quicker route to bankruptcy. I usually advise you pay COBRA before you pay your mortgage. There's nothing more important than your health.

➲ You can possibly speed things up by calling the plan administrator yourself as soon as you have a qualifying event and letting him or her know. Call HR and push them to get the notice out.

➲ If you have upcoming surgery, ongoing medical expenses, or other health issues, let the former employer know time is of the essence in getting you covered.

➲ Having the employer pay all or part of COBRA costs is frequently something you can negotiate as part of a severance package.

Can I Sue for Constructive Discharge?

Sometimes, people come to me and say they want to sue for constructive discharge. There's no such cause of action or claim. Constructive discharge is where an employee quits work for good cause. If you would have a case against your employer had they fired you under the same circumstances (workers' compensation retaliation, retaliation for complaining about discrimination, whistle-blower retaliation, and adverse action discrimination claims, to name a few) then you will also probably have a case against them if a court finds you were constructively discharged.

Most courts are reluctant to find constructively discharge. The standard is usually that no reasonable employee would have tolerated the conditions of employment. For instance, I've seen sexual harassment cases as extreme as rape that weren't found to have been so intolerable that the circumstances constituted constructive discharge by the employer.

For unemployment purposes, if the company cuts your pay, changes your job duties in a major way, changes your shift, or transfers you to a new location, that may be enough to be deemed cause attributable to the employer. You'd better be sure before you quit if you want to qualify for unemployment. Sometimes the unemployment office will have Websites to go to or someone to call for information. Be sure of your rights before you quit.

Donna's Tips

⊃ If your working conditions are intolerable, for heaven's sake look for another job. Don't quit until you have another job lined up. It's easier to get a job when you have a job.

⊃ If working conditions are intolerable due to discrimination, sexual harassment, failure to pay wages, or something protected by law, complain to HR in writing before you quit and give the company a chance to correct the situation.

⊃ If the work situation is dangerous (rape, assault, unsafe conditions), get the heck out of there. No lawsuit or potential suit is worth your safety.

My Former Employer Sent Me Something by Certified Mail. Should I Refuse It?

Sometimes people proudly announce to me that their employer is trying to send them something, but they refuse to sign for it. I really don't understand. What do you think it is? A snake? They might be sending you something important like COBRA paperwork or a termination letter that will help you file for unemployment. Maybe you left something in the office and they are sending it to you.

For goodness sake, sign for it. You must know what it is and if there are any deadlines.

Donna's Tips

⊃ Never turn down certified mail. Ignoring it doesn't make it go away.

⊃ Read what you are sent. If there are deadlines (for example, to turn in your COBRA paperwork), you must comply or lose your right to file.

I Think I'm About to Be Laid Off. How Do I Prepare?

The signs are there. Your boss won't look you in the eye. You're directed to write down everything you do and how you do it. A new person started a week ago and you've been asked to train him. You're on your way out.

Although this is a stressful time, it's also an opportunity to prepare. Here's what you should do before the axe falls:

Gather Evidence: Remember how I said to take good notes if you thought you were being singled out due to race, age, sex, national origin, or another protected category? Well, now's the time to assure they're up to date and out of the office. Don't have them in your desk drawer when the summons comes. You may never get them back. Now is also the time to copy any documents that might help a lawyer: evidence of discrimination, time records showing overtime worked—whatever you think might show you have a claim against the company.

Polish Your Resume: It's been awhile since you updated the old CV. Look through your records to see what projects you worked on, kudos you got, great comments about your work.

Gather Your Kudos: Have you gotten thank-you notes, nice letters, awards, or great reviews? Copy them. Take any plaques, certificates, and awards home.

Look at Your File: Get a copy of your personnel file if you can: any contracts, reviews, disciplines, awards, continuing education certificates—anything you might need.

Copy the Handbook and Policies: Copy anything relating to insurance, retirement, benefits, severance, termination, layoffs, and anything else that might be useful.

With a little advance preparation, you can ease your transition and hopefully have everything you need if you are let go.

Donna's Tips

➲ Be discreet. Don't empty out your office one day. They'll say you quit.

➲ Don't tell coworkers you think you're about to be fired. You might bring something to pass that isn't planned.

➲ Do your best work. Don't give them any excuses. Keep a good attitude, even if it hurts to smile.

Can My Company Give Me a Bad Reference?

Your employer called you incompetent. Said you aren't eligible for rehire. You're hopping mad. It's a lie! Slander. Libel. You must be able to sue, right? Meh. Probably not. Slander and libel are types of defamation. Defamation is where your former employer makes a false statement of fact about you to someone other than you that damages your reputation. Most references, even bad ones, probably aren't defamation.

Here's what you should know about job references:

Knowingly False: Some states have statutes protecting job references from defamation claims, but even then the employer cannot give out knowingly false information. A statement that you were an embezzler, Ponzi schemer, or pedophile made when they knew it was false, is probably not protected.

Opinion: Statements of opinion are not defamation. If the employer says you didn't fit into the corporate culture or didn't have the job knowledge they wanted, these may be opinion, not fact. Statements like "In my opinion, she was a thief" are still defamation.

Donna's Tips

⊃ Defamation claims against employers can be tough. Many judges don't like them.

⊃ Sometimes a cease and desist letter will accomplish more than a lawsuit. Getting the defamer to stop the statements might be more valuable to you.

⊃ Professional reference-checking companies you can find on-line will pretend to be potential employers. When in doubt, hire one and find out exactly what is being said about you.

Do I Have to Give Notice When I Quit?

There's no law requiring you give any notice to employers when you leave. However, giving notice is the normal courtesy when leaving all but the worst situations. Even if you have a contract requiring notice, I've never heard of any court requiring anyone to continue working against their will. Here's what you should know about giving notice:

Firing: I've heard many cases of employees giving notice, then the employer turning around and saying: "Leave now." Although this is a jerk move, and encourages other employees not to give notice, it's not illegal. Be prepared for this possibility, especially if you work for a jerk. Don't be caught flat-footed by relying on those last few weeks of pay. Have a plan for what you will do if they don't let you stay. Maybe the new employer will let you start earlier.

Vacation: Many people try to use their vacation when giving notice. Most employers won't let you do this. If you really need to take that pre-paid vacation, come back to work after vacation, and then give notice. Otherwise, you might be taking an unpaid vacation.

Breach of Contract: If your contract requires notice, it's conceivable your employer could sue for breach. They must prove you damaged them. I would argue there's no such thing as indentured servitude. Courts generally won't make you work against your will, but it's possible you would have to pay damages.

Do Your Job: Don't use your notice period to slack off or, worse, copy company information for your new job. Leave on good terms. It's a small world. Your boss might just end up at your new company next year. Surprise!

Donna's Tips

➲ Giving notice makes sense. If you leave on bad terms, guess who will slam you in references?

➲ If the employer fires people who give notice, then either don't bother with notice or be ready for the heave-ho.

➲ If they do fire you after giving notice, you might qualify for unemployment or have other rights, such as breach of contract or even discrimination.

Am I Entitled to Severance? Should I Sign a Severance Agreement?

There is no legal entitlement to severance unless you have a contract saying so, or if your employer has a published severance policy. However, many employers offer severance to you when you are fired or laid off.

Here are some things to consider:

Understand It: If you don't understand everything in the agreement, have a lawyer review it. You may lose rights you haven't considered or may agree to something that will cost you more than the amount of severance.

Pension: Do you have a pension? How is it dealt with in the agreement? Many agreements contain releases under ERISA, the law that governing pensions. Don't accidentally give up your pension rights. If you had an employer-matched 401(k) and are not vested, you are probably losing the employer contribution to your 401(k).

Non-Compete: Did you have a non-compete agreement? If not, and the employer is adding one, it may limit your ability to get a new job. If the time restriction is longer than the number of weeks of severance, it is probably not worth signing the agreement unless you are going into an entirely new field. If you had a non-compete agreement, make sure you understand your existing limitations before you sign a severance agreement. You are likely reaffirming those restrictions in a severance agreement, so may lose your defenses to the non-competition provisions. Some employers try to add restrictions you did not have, such as making the restrictions longer or for a larger geographic area. Some know they had an unenforceable agreement and use the severance agreement to put in place an enforceable provision.

Release: You are likely giving up all claims you have against the employer. If you have a workers' compensation, discrimination, or overtime claim, signing the agreement means you are giving those up. Is the release mutual? If the employer wants you to release them from any claims, they should also release you. I have seen unscrupulous employers have employees sign releases, then turn around and sue for alleged wrongdoing on the job. Mutual releases assure any claims are released by both sides. In banking, or other financial arenas, the employer will want an exception for undiscovered financial fraud/embezzlement, which is okay. If they know about it at the time of the agreement, they should be willing to release it or give up their right to a release so the employee can assert any defenses or counterclaims they have.

Confidentiality: Is confidentiality mutual? Employers want the severance agreement to be confidential. If the employer doesn't have to keep it confidential, they may get cute and say things to references like "I must look at the agreement to see what I'm allowed to say." Protect yourself so they can't disclose the agreement to potential employers.

Non-Disparagement: You don't want this employer to be able to say bad things to potential employers or to customers, coworkers, or others in the community. If they want non-disparagement to be mutual, to keep you from bad-mouthing them, agree. It is worth the peace of mind to know they won't make negative comments keeping you from future employment.

Insurance: Many employers will pay some or all of your COBRA payments to tide you over while you are unemployed. Understand what will happen to your insurance benefits.

Stock: Do you have stock options, stock appreciation rights, or other similar rights? Make you're not giving up valuable rights. If you were about to vest, see if the employer will agree to vest your rights. If you were fired to keep you from vesting, you may have claims against the employer.

Leverage: Do you have any potential claims against the employer? Potential claims may give you leverage to negotiate a severance package if it is not offered or to negotiate a better package.

Donna's Tips

⊃　Some claim to be offended by a request to make a release mutual and say: "What did you do that you need to be released from?" The answer, of course, is "What did *you* do that you need to be released from?"

⊃　You may have claims against the employer you never thought about before.

Can They Take Away My Vested Benefits?

If you sign a release in your severance agreement, make sure you aren't releasing vested benefits. Any release that doesn't contain an exemption for your vested benefits may enable your former employer to get out of paying them. Here are some benefits to be concerned about:

401(k): Your 401(k) is yours, so it's unlikely that any release could affect it. If any employer contributions are vested, they are sitting in your account, and the employer would likely be unable to touch them. However, any unvested benefits can be rescinded, so beware. If your release doesn't say that your 401(k) will be fully vested, those unvested contributions will disappear.

Stock Options: If you have any unvested options, they are gone if you sign a release. You might even lose vested options. Look at your option agreement to see if you will lose them anyway once your employment is terminated, or if you should fight to keep them.

Stock: Stock is property, not a "claim" that you can release. I've still seen employers vigorously argue that an employee released stock by signing a general release. This argument is likely a loser, but be aware of it. Another concern is a stock issue that says the company can buy it back at some ridiculous valuation if you are no longer an employee. Review any documents sent with your stock issue, such as any shareholder agreements, to determine your rights before you sign. If you have unvested stock rights, they will likely be gone.

Pension: Be careful of signing a release of all ERISA claims. You might accidentally give up your pension. Make sure the release says you aren't giving up vested pension benefits if you're one of the lucky few who still have a real pension plan.

Other Benefits: Employers have all kinds of benefits, so know what yours are and understand what will happen to them. Stock appreciation rights, life insurance, disability insurance, and other benefits may disappear when you sign a release.

Donna's Tips

⊃ Don't assume that "vested" means it's yours. Always protect your vested rights and be cautious of what you sign.

⊃ Read anything that comes with any stock, options, or other benefits. Keep copies somewhere that you will be able to find later. These documents are issued for a reason. Understand your rights if you are fired or leave.

Does the Company Have to Give Notice of a Mass Layoff?

The Worker Adjustment and Retraining Notification (WARN) Act says certain employers must give notice in advance of a mass layoff. Here's what you should know about the WARN Act:

Employers Covered: If your employer has at least 100 employees and it isn't a government entity, it is covered.

Employees: Employers don't need to count employees who have worked less than six months of the last 12, or employees who work less than 20 hours per week toward their 100 total employees. However, if the employer has 100 or more employees, including part-time workers, who work at least 4,000 hours per week if you total them together and don't count overtime, they are covered.

Notice: The employer must give at least 60 days' notice of certain layoffs and closings if they are covered.

Covered Layoffs: If 50 to 499 employees are laid off during any 30-day period at a single employment site (or if there are multiple related layoffs during a 90-day period), and if the total laid off employees are at least 33 percent of the employer's workforce where the layoff will occur, they must give notice if the layoff will result in an employment loss for more than six months. If the layoff affects 500 or more workers, they must give notice of layoffs that will result in job loss for more than six months, no matter what percentage of the workforce is affected.

Covered Closings: If the company is closing a facility or operating unit for more than six months, or if 50 or more employees will lose their jobs during any 30-day period at a single jobsite, they must give notice. This doesn't apply if it's a temporary facility or if the workers were hired to complete a specific job.

Less Notice Allowed: If the company is faltering, there are unforeseeable business circumstances, or there's a natural disaster, the company may be allowed to give less notice.

Who Gets Notice?: Employees or their representatives, if there's a union, must get notice. The chief elected officials of your local government also get notice. If notice goes to your representative, the representative must get the notice to you.

Remedy: You can sue on behalf of yourself or you can file a class action. Your representatives or elected officials can also sue. The employer would have to pay back pay and benefits for the period of the violation, up to 60 days. This may be reduced by the period of any notice that was given, and any voluntary payments the employer made to you, such as severance. If the government sues for you, they can recover $500/day of violation, unless the company pays its liability to each employee within three weeks after the closing or layoff. You can also recover your attorney's fees and costs if you win. You can't, unfortunately, stop the layoff or closing altogether.

Donna's Tips

- If you get a WARN Act notice, read it carefully. Make your plans to find another job right away. The notice will also tell you if you have any bumping rights (the right to take a lower-level job held by another employee).
- Truthfully, unless you are part of a class action or you can convince the union or an elected official to sue for you, your time is probably better spent job hunting than suing.

Crisis Scenarios Post-Employment

Scenario 1

You're fired. The HR manager shows up in your office with security and escorts you out. You ask why. He says: "We don't have to give a reason."

Do you:

    ❑ a. Demand a written notice of termination giving the reasons you've been fired?

    ❑ b. Demand to say goodbye to your coworkers?

    ❑ c. Leave quietly, but ask first to be allowed to pack up your belongings?

If you answered a:

Unless you live in a state requiring written notice of termination, you aren't entitled to this. Few employers give written notice these days. However, if they won't give a reason, it's harder for them to claim a reason later if you sue for, say, discrimination. Their refusal might create an issue of fact that lets you get to a jury.

If you answered b:

They probably won't let you. They don't want you to make a scene. There's no right to say goodbye before you go.

If you answered c:

You behaved with class. Hopefully they'll let you collect your things. If they do, make sure to get your briefcase, purse, personal photos, awards, and personal items. If you left your notes on all the discriminatory comments or sexual harassment that occurred in your desk drawer, they may not let you take it. That's why you keep it at home, in your purse, or in your briefcase. Don't try to copy stuff from your computer or take company documents. You'll get accused of stealing trade secrets.

Scenario 2

After you leave, HR pesters you to come in for an exit interview. Do you:

    ❑ a. Ignore them? You don't work there anymore.

    ❑ b. Go and see what they have to say?

    ❑ c. Go and complain about any grievances you have against your former supervisor and the company?

If you answered a:

That's what I'd do. Screw 'em.

If you answered b:

You can do this, but they might try to get you to sign a severance agreement, get you to admit to some wrongdoing, or say that it was a good place to work (or they might claim you said this) to evade later discrimination or other claims. Be careful what you say, and take good notes. Don't sign anything without reading and understanding. If you don't understand it, take it to a lawyer.

If you answered c:

You're probably wasting your time. They consider you a disgruntled ex-employee. If you do this, put it in writing and limit your complaint to illegal practices such as discrimination.

Scenario 3

You get a certified package from your former employer. Do you:

- ❏ a. Refuse it? You don't have to take anything from them anymore.
- ❏ b. Sign for it and open it immediately? Read any contents carefully.
- ❏ c. Sign for it, then burn it? You don't care what they have to say.

If you answered a:

Dumb move. Ignoring it doesn't make it go away. You're probably getting something you should know about.

If you answered b:

This is exactly what you should do. You're probably getting your COBRA notice to continue your health insurance coverage. Even if it's a letter threatening to sue you for violating your non-compete, claiming you stole something, or something else unpleasant, you should know about it.

If you answered c:

You just burned your COBRA notice. Good luck being uninsured.

Scenario 4

You think you're about to be fired. Do you:

❑ a. Start an anonymous blog and post all the dirt you have on the company?

❑ b. Pack up your notes and documents that support your discrimination, overtime, or whistle-blower claim and take them home?

❑ c. Start looking quietly for another job?

If you answered a:

It might be cathartic, but you may get caught and give them the excuse they need to fire you, or sue you for giving away confidential information or defamation.

If you answered b:

Definitely do this. Don't have your proof in your desk drawer when they escort you out. It will disappear faster than Rice Krispie treats at a 10-year-old's birthday party.

If you answered c:

Even if you answered b, you should start doing this discreetly. It's way easier to get a job if you have one.

Scenario 5

You start looking for a job and have great interviews. They say they'll check your references and get back to you. You never hear from any of them again. When you call, they are abrupt and say they'll call if they are interested. Do you:

❑ a. Hire a professional reference-checking company to find out what your former employer is saying?

❑ b. Sue them for defamation? They must be saying something really bad.

❑ c. Do a background check on yourself? Google your name and get a free credit check to make sure nothing weird is turning up.

If you answered a:

It is possible they're saying something bad, but you don't know. Times are tough, so it's possible you're just not getting picked. It's best to be sure what they're saying so you can tailor your interview answers around it, and so you can pursue a defamation claim if they're giving false information.

If you answered b:

You have no proof. If they're giving out tepid references, are saying you weren't a good fit, or saying something that's pure opinion, you probably don't have a defamation claim. It's your burden to prove what they said, who they said it to, and that you were damaged. Get proof.

If you answered c:

You might want to do this in addition to a. It could be that something else is causing you to lose out on jobs.

Scenario 6

You hate your job and can't stand it anymore. You are going to quit. Do you:

❏ a. Walk out without notice and scream: "Screw you guys, I'm going home."?

❏ b. Give at least two weeks' written notice?

❏ c. Send an e-mail to all your customers and coworkers explaining in detail why you're leaving and that it's a horrible place?

If you answered a:

Uh, boy. Is this tempting, or what? But if you leave without notice and make a scene to boot, you've blown your chance at any good references and you've burned bridges.

If you answered b:

You're a class act. If your contract or custom in your industry require even more notice, give it. Assure a smooth transition. Your coworkers or boss may end up at your new place of employment one day.

If you answered c:

You've made enemies for life. Worse, they might sue you for tortious interference with their employees or business relationships. It's not worth it.

Scenario 7

Same as scenario 6, except the past three employees who gave notice were escorted out immediately. Do you:

❑ a. Walk out on your last day? Don't say anything or tell them what you're doing.

❑ b. Pack your things a little at a time? Take them out when you leave every day. On your last day, put a resignation letter on the desk of the HR person or your boss, and explain why you didn't give notice.

❑ c. Give notice anyway? It's still the classy thing to do.

If you answered a:

You should still tell them you're quitting. Just wait until you're ready. If you can't afford to be unemployed for two weeks, give your resignation at the end of your last day.

If you answered b:

This is about the best you're going to be able to do if you work for jerks. Pack up so it's not very noticeable. Pack photos and big items on your last day. Walk them to the car, then walk back and hand in your resignation.

If you answered c:

Yes, this is the class thing to do. But you work for jerks with no class. If you can afford to be out of work for a couple weeks, do it. Otherwise, wait.

Scenario 8

You're fired. Your boss shoves a paper in front of you and demands that you sign. Do you:

❑ a. Sign? It doesn't matter anymore.

❑ b. Tell her you want to take it to an attorney to review?

❑ c. Review it carefully? If you understand and agree, sign. Get a copy.

If you answered a:

You may have just signed a release of all claims you had against this employer, or have agreed not to work for a competitor for a year or two. At the very least, you may have signed a resignation or admitted to wrongdoing that keeps you from getting unemployment.

If you answered b:

You're pretty upset and not thinking clearly. Even if you don't actually go to a lawyer, this will buy you time to review and think about it. When in doubt about what it means, take it to a lawyer in your state.

If you answered c:

If you're savvy, you might be okay to do this. However, you're upset. You may miss something important. I advise against signing most things at a termination interview unless it's just a paper acknowledging that you've received notice, or something equally basic.

Scenario 9

You've decided to sign your severance agreement and walk away. You have vested pension benefits. The agreement doesn't say what happens to them. Do you:

❑ a. Sign? They can't take away vested benefits.

❑ b. Read the paperwork that came with the agreement to see what the company says will happen?

❑ c. Ask the company to add to the release: "This release does not apply to employee's vested pension benefits."?

If you answered a:

Wrong! Although most companies won't try this, if it says you're releasing ERISA claims you might lose pension rights. Be careful.

If you answered b:

Sometimes you get a package with the severance agreement saying what happens to each benefit. If this package satisfactorily explains what happens to your pension, you're probably okay. However, the agreement probably says it's the entire agreement and you're not relying on anything but what's in the agreement. That makes this move somewhat risky.

If you answered c:

This is what I would prefer to do. Better safe than sorry. If they won't do it but say you aren't giving up your pension, attach a cover letter confirming this and say you are relying on this information. Tell them that, if you are incorrect, they should advise you immediately so you can revoke your acceptance.

Scenario 10

You are called into HR and told you're being laid off in two weeks. Your entire division is shutting down. Hundreds of people are affected. Do you:

❑ a. Ask about severance or notice pay?

❑ b. Contact your city or county mayor about pursuing a claim against the company?

❑ c. File a union grievance?

If you answered a:

This is my best suggestion. They may have to give you 60 days' notice under the WARN Act. Rather than jumping right into pursuing legal remedies, see if you can get them to do the right thing first. You might want to give them a copy of the WARN Act.

If you answered b:

It's possible they might actually do something if the layoff is big enough. However, government employees are distracted and busy, so I wouldn't count on them.

If you answered c:

If you have a union, bring it to their attention. They could pursue claims on behalf of everyone being laid off. Though you can pursue individual claims under the WARN Act, it might be better to be part of a class action.

Post-Employment Blues:

Unemployment, Defamation, Non-Competes, Confidentiality, Interference With New Employment

Can My Employer Enforce My Confidentiality Agreement?

Before you started working, or during your employment, your employer might have handed you a "confidentiality agreement" or something similar to sign. Hopefully you read it carefully before you signed, because these frequently contain non-compete agreements. You might have signed away your right to go work for a competitor for one or two years.

Employers are entitled to protect information that is truly confidential. If they get it off the Internet, or it is on their website, in printed brochures, or on publicly available sources, it's not confidential. But if the employer makes an effort to keep it confidential (marking it "Confidential," locking it up, making efforts to keep it from competitors), you probably must keep it confidential.

When you leave, you can't copy or e-mail yourself the employer's confidential information, particularly if you've signed a confidentiality agreement.

Donna's Tips

➲ Don't believe anyone who tells you these agreements are never enforced. They're wrong.

➲ Failing to read or understand a contract is never an excuse to evade complying.

⊃ If you're bound by an agreement, make sure you have a copy.
   Some employers resist giving a copy, which I don't understand. How can an employee comply with an agreement if
   he or she doesn't have a copy? If your employer resists, tell
   them you want it to make sure you don't violate it accidentally.
   Hopefully, they'll give it to you. If they claim you've violated
   an agreement you don't have a copy of, ask for it or have your
   lawyer ask for a copy. Don't just believe them if they claim
   you've signed. Lots of employers assume everyone has signed
   when they haven't. Some even (dare I say?) lie.

My Employer Is Bad-Mouthing Me. Can I Sue for Defamation?

References aren't the only place you may be bad-mouthed. Defamation
is where your employer or former employer makes a false statement of
fact about you to someone other than you damaging your reputation. If
you start a business or are in sales, and they bad-mouth you to customers, slam you at conferences, or post nasty stuff on your public profiles,
you might have a defamation claim. Here's what you need to know about
workplace defamation:

Qualified Privilege: Employers have a qualified privilege—that is,
one that can be overcome—to conduct an investigation of employee
wrongdoing. For instance, if someone complains of age discrimination,
the employer's human resources person, the employer's attorney, and
the named witnesses can speak about the investigation and will probably
be protected. There are some ways to overcome a qualified privilege,
so you'll want to talk to an attorney even if you think the statement was
privileged.

Publication: The information must have been "published" to a third
party, which only means that it had to be said to someone other than you.
Some states consider statements made inside the company not to have
been published. A statement to you about you is never defamation unless
others were present to hear it.

Absolute Privilege: Some communications can never be the subject of
a defamation case no matter how knowingly false. These may include statements made in a legal proceeding, to police, to administrative agencies,

and by government officials in the scope of their employment. I say "may" because this can vary by state and be fact-specific.

Opinion: Statements of opinion are not defamation.

Donna's Tips

➲ Corporations can be defamed just the same as individuals. If you have a blog or Website, or make statements disparaging the company or their products, be careful to get your facts right.

➲ Sometimes a cease and desist letter will accomplish more than a lawsuit. Getting the defamer to stop the statements might be more valuable to you.

➲ If you are thinking about filing a defamation claim against an individual, make sure the person has assets that will make them collectible. Broke defendants can be frustrating when you try to collect.

Do I Need to Make an Administrative Claim Before I Can Sue?

Administrative claims are ones you must make with a government agency instead of a court. There are all kinds of administrative claims in employment law. Here are some of the reasons you might need to make an administrative claim:

Discrimination: If you have a discrimination claim, you must file a charge of discrimination with the EEOC and/or your state human rights agency before you can file suit. If you don't, you forever lose your right to sue for discrimination.

Unemployment: If you lose your job, your state's unemployment compensation agency is where you'll apply for unemployment benefits.

Whistle-Blowing: There are zillions of federal and state whistle-blower protections. Many of them have some administrative hoops you must jump through before you can bring a lawsuit, and some only allow administrative claims.

Sexual Orientation Discrimination: Federal law doesn't protect against sexual orientation discrimination or harassment, so each state and local government that allows such claims has different processes. Some only allow you to bring your claims through administrative agencies, and some allow a suit only after bringing administrative claims.

Grievances: Some private employers, most government entities, and most union shops have a grievance process through which you can appeal unfair termination or discipline. These procedures are sometimes being used as a sword by employers to prevent employees from bringing lawsuits. The argument is that the employee failed to exhaust their administrative remedies first. If you do have a grievance procedure available, contact your union rep and maybe a labor lawyer.

Sometimes you get caught up in a catch-22 situation. The union pursues the grievance, then fails to advise you that you can appeal it. You try to bring a discrimination or whistle-blower claim, only to be told that you forever gave up your right to sue by failing to bring an appeal that would have been futile. If you bring the appeal knowing it's futile, you can be sanctioned for a frivolous action.

Or, you'll bring a grievance and try to raise an issue such as discrimination, only to be told it's not a proper subject of a grievance. You try to bring it in court and are told you lost your right to sue because you didn't raise it in the grievance.

If you bring it in the grievance, then you may well lose. The employer frequently is the one who picks the hearing examiners or arbitrators, and these processes can sometimes be biased toward the employer. If you lose, the courts say the matter is "res judicata"—that is, already decided, and you lose your right to sue.

Confused? I'm pretty sure you're meant to be. If Congress wanted to fix this ridiculous situation it could.

Donna's Tips

➲ Some claims you don't have to bring through an administrative agency first are unpaid wages, overtime, FMLA violations, and some state and local claims.

➲ It's not all bad to file with an administrative agency. The process is usually quicker and less expensive than court, and you may get helpful evidence you can use in court later.

I Got a Letter Saying I Violated My Duty of Loyalty. Is There Such a Thing?

Although the law imposes zero duty of loyalty requiring your employer to be loyal to you, as an employee you have a duty of loyalty to your employer. Once you leave, you can be as disloyal as you want (as long as you don't have a contract saying otherwise). Employers who can't enforce or don't have non-compete agreements use the duty of loyalty to attack former employees and bully them post-employment. Here's what you should know about your duty of loyalty:

Non-Compete: Even though you don't have a non-compete agreement, you can't actually form a competing company or work for a competitor and compete while you're still employed.

Preparing to Compete: You can prepare to form a competing company or to work for a competitor while you're still employed. However, you can't do anything harming your current employer. That means you probably can't solicit customers and employees to leave, can't give the employer misleading information, can't steer corporate opportunities to your new business, and can't steer the company away from business you plan to take.

Trade Secrets: You can never steal trade secrets from your employer. Don't copy their confidential financial or customer information to use in your new business.

Looking for Another Job: You can look for another job while you're still employed.

Not Working: You can't declare an in-cube sabbatical and start working on your new company while getting paid by your current employer.

Damages: If a court finds you breached your duty of loyalty, your employer must prove damages. They might claim that you shouldn't have been paid while you were working against their interests and demand a refund of your wages, ask the court to make you pay them all your profits earned while you owed them a duty, or ask for punitive damages or even an injunction to stop you.

Donna's Tips

- ⟶ If you're planning on leaving your employer, do it cleanly and fairly. Don't steal, cheat, lie, or defraud your employer, even if you hate them.

⊃ While you're working, don't try to get customers to stop
   doing business with the company.

⊃ You probably still have the right to blow the whistle on illegal
   behavior even though you have a duty of loyalty.

How Do I Get Out of My Non-Compete Agreement?

Your employer will try to enforce your non-compete agreement when
you leave. Most employees don't have the will or the resources to fight non-
competes. Many employees think that, just because an employer forced
them to sign the agreement or they were fired, they are not bound by their
non-compete agreement. That's just not true. Continued employment
is valid consideration for a non-compete agreement in some states, and
almost all will enforce some non-compete provisions. That doesn't mean
you can't get out of yours if you're willing to fight.

What usually happens is the employer sends a letter to your new employer and you, threatens to sue both, and you get fired from your new
job, even where you told the new employer about the non-compete. That's
because, unless you have a contract with the new employer saying you can
only be fired for cause, and the non-compete is known to the employer and
is not cause, they can fire you at will in all but one state.

Can your employer enforce your non-compete? Maybe. Can they out-
last you financially if they sue you? Almost certainly. Do you have rights?
Absolutely.

Here are some legal arguments you may have to defeat your non-compete:

Employer Breaches the Contract: If the non-compete provision is in
an employment contract spelling out compensation, insurance, and other
conditions of employment, go through the contract line-by-line. If the employer breached the agreement by failing to pay all compensation due,
fulfill the insurance requirements, or meet another obligation, you may be
relieved of all obligations under the contract.

No Legitimate Interest to Enforce: Many employers attempt to over-
reach their legitimate business interests, and this is one of the most common mistakes. For instance, an employer has no legitimate interest in
enforcing a non-compete against low-level employees such as receptionists
and clerical employees. An employer that manufactures computer widgets

for airplanes has no legitimate interest in preventing you from working on widgets for telephones. An employer phasing out of an area has no legitimate interest in preventing you from working in that area. An employer that abandons a customer, area of business, or product has no legitimate interest in what it abandoned. What might be legitimate interests in your state are trade secrets; valuable confidential business or professional information; substantial relationships with specific prospective or existing customers, patients, or clients; goodwill associated with an ongoing business or professional practice (by way of a trademark, geographic location, or marketing/trade area); and extraordinary or specialized training.

Restriction Is Too Long: Your state non-compete statutes determine what length is reasonable. For instance, less than six months may be presumed valid, and more than two years presumed invalid. In between, the employer must prove the length is reasonable. However, courts may assume agreements up to your state's maximum are reasonable. Anything over your state's set maximum is a hurdle for the employer to overcome.

The So-Called Confidential Information Is Readily Available to the Public: Many companies get sales leads from public sources. Phone books, professional directories, the Internet, and notification services are sources available to anyone. An employer that claims they are protecting valuable secret client sources must prove the information was not available to everyone else in the industry. Existing customer lists or unique sources may well be protected, but chamber of commerce directories are probably not.

Public Health or Safety Would Not Be Served: This primarily applies to doctors, nurses, and specialized scientific and health fields. If there is a shortage of people in a specialty or geographic area, the employer probably cannot enforce a non-compete even if all the other requirements are met. If you are one of 10 brain surgeons in the country who can perform a particular procedure, your employer probably can't prevent you from saving people's lives.

Assume your non-compete agreement is enforceable, and don't sign unless you can live with the restrictions. An employee with the time, will, and resources to fight can frequently limit or eliminate their non-compete provisions.

An employer that tries to enforce a non-compete and fails may end up paying the attorney's fees and costs of the prevailing employee, and will sometimes be paying money damages to the employee for tortious inter-ference with an employment relationship if they cost the employee a job.

Donna's Tips

⊃ Does it stink that companies can force you to sign a non-compete and use it as essentially indentured servitude? Yes. I see cases all the time of bully bosses using non-competes to force employees to stay under terrible conditions. Or worse, cases where employees quit their great job based on promises and were presented with a non-compete after they started the new job. Within a month, the new employer uploads all their valuable contacts into the database, then fires the poor employee, then says the employee can't work in their field for a year or two. Do courts enforce such despicable schemes? Sometimes.

⊃ If you're leaving a job and you have a non-compete, look at the agreement to see which state's law applies, and get a law-yer in that state to take a look. If no state is specified, then it's probably the state where you work for the employer. A written agreement with the new employer to defend and pay you even if a court issues an injunction will protect you.

⊃ If you get sued to enforce a non-compete, you *must* contact an employment attorney in the state where you're sued imme-diately to defend yourself or you will lose your new job, have a money judgment against you, and waive any defenses to the agreement.

⊃ The laws need to change, so call your state legislators and complain. Better yet, write them.

Can My Employer Enforce a Non-Solicitation Agreement?

Non-solicitation agreements are where you agree not to solicit the company's customers, employees, vendors, or other key people to stop do-ing business with the company for a certain amount of time after you leave.

Whereas there are lots of defenses to non-compete agreements, judges do tend to like to enforce non-solicitation agreements. The employer must have a legitimate interest to protect, and if the employer breaches their contract with you by failing to pay you wages or another breach, it may be a defense to their ability to enforce the agreement.

The main argument I see against enforcement of non-solicitation agreements is antitrust. Companies can't have an agreement for the sole purpose of limiting competition. Without trade secrets or other legitimate interests to protect, non-solicitation and non-compete agreements may well violate antitrust laws.

Donna's Tips

- ⊃ Even if you manage to convince a judge to toss out your non-compete, he or she may still prohibit you from soliciting the company's customers to leave.

- ⊃ There's usually no restriction on customers who voluntarily follow you. If customers find out you have joined a new company, your state law may allow them to follow you if you haven't solicited them.

- ⊃ If customers are easily found in the phone book or trade directories, they might be fair game to anyone.

I Took the Customer List and Copied a Bunch of Stuff Before I Left, and Now They Say I Stole Trade Secrets. Can They Sue Me?

It's common for companies to have employees sign an agreement saying they won't take trade secrets or confidential information when they leave. Many employees wrongly assume that, if they never signed an agreement, they can take their employer's customer list or other confidential information, and use it to form their own business or give it to their new employer. Whether or not you signed an agreement regarding your company's trade secrets, every employee is affected by trade secret law.

Most company information is not a trade secret. Even if you did sign a confidentiality agreement, some information isn't protected. Here is what you should know about trade secrets:

Independent Value: It's a trade secret if the very fact of it being unknown to competitors makes it have independent value. In other words, if it is something a competitor would value, then it might be a trade secret. If you are the safe-keeper of the KFC secret recipe or know the formula for Coca Cola, it's a no-brainer that you have a trade secret. But competitors might find other, less obvious information valuable, such as client lists, manuals, or pricing.

Kept Confidential: Your company will almost always claim their customer list is a trade secret. Yet many companies brag about customers on their Websites. Some even put their whole customer list, pricing, brochures, and manuals out there on the Web. If the company put it on the Web or in public, it can't be a trade secret. If they put their "secret recipe" into a charity cookbook, goodbye trade secret. If they apply for a patent, the information becomes public record and is no longer a trade secret.

Not Available Through Public Sources: If the way your company gets its business is through cold-calling the yellow pages, business directories, chamber of commerce listings, or Google, they probably can't protect their customer list. If, for instance, you sell grommets to shoe manufacturers, your potential client list is a finite one. If you search for "shoe manufacturer" on the Web and can generate a potential client list, you're allowed to do so when you work for a competitor.

Not Available for Purchase: If your company gets leads from a purchased source, the leads are not a trade secret. If everyone in your industry gets leads from an e-mail alert that they pay to subscribe to and the first to contact the customer or the one with the best price wins, that's treated the same as a publicly available source. It isn't a trade secret.

Not Ascertainable: Just because the company keeps it under lock and key and thought of it first still doesn't necessarily make it a trade secret. For instance, if the company compiles a "secret database" of leads, but their compilation consists of buying yellow pages, Dun and Bradstreet listings, and a chamber of commerce directory, and merging them into one list, it's not hard for a competitor to come up with the same list. The information must be something they used considerable time and expense to put together, and that competitors wouldn't be able to figure out on their own.

Non-Competes and Trade Secrets: Non-compete agreements can only be used to protect a legitimate interest of the employer, such as trade secrets. The one thing a non-compete agreement can never be used for is to prevent competition—that's antitrust and a violation of federal and most state laws. If your non-compete agreement says its purpose is to protect the company's trade secrets, then the company can only enforce it if you had access to actual trade secrets.

Donna's Tips

⊃ If you had access to a trade secret, you can't blog or tweet about it, e-mail it to yourself and use it, give it to your new employer, or give or sell it to a friend.

⊃ Some companies use an employee's access to trade secrets to bully them into not working for a competitor or going out on their own. When the employee announces she's leaving, the company lawyer sends a letter threatening the employee with a trade secret suit. Many employees get scared and stay or get jobs outside their industry because they can't afford to fight or lose their jobs. Just because you had access to a trade secret doesn't automatically mean you can't work in a competing business. Most company information isn't a trade secret.

⊃ If you signed a confidentiality agreement or had access to something you think might be a trade secret, get advice from an employment lawyer in your state about your rights and responsibilities before you accept a job from a competitor or copy the information to use after you leave.

I Got a New Job and My Former Employer Sent Them a Letter That Got Me Fired. Can I Sue?

If your former employer interferes with your new employment without any legal justification, you might have a claim called "tortious interference." Tortious interference is where you have an employment relationship the former employer knows about, and they intentionally and unjustifiably interfere with that relationship, causing you damages. If you get fired due to false information or a claim that you have an unenforceable non-compete agreement, the former employer that interferes might be liable.

If your former employer gives out false information, such as saying you are a thief, then you might also have a claim for defamation.

On the other hand, if you have a non-compete agreement and the employer is just trying to enforce it, and they send a letter in good faith advising your new employer of the agreement, they're probably allowed to do it. If the agreement has expired, if it doesn't say what they claim it does, or if they know it isn't enforceable, then they might be tortiously interfering.

Donna's Tips

- ⊃ If you get a nasty-gram from your former employer or their lawyer, don't ignore it. If you know what they are saying is false, respond calmly and professionally to them, and let them know what is correct. For instance, if they claim you solicited a customer that you never heard of, let them know their information is wrong. If you don't respond, they'll assume the worst.

- ⊃ If your employer gets a letter like this, ask them for a copy. Review it carefully. Ask them for time to sort it out if they seem like they want to fire you.

- ⊃ Sometimes a letter from a lawyer explaining why they are wrong will get them to back off. Sometimes, they'll persist even if they know they are wrong.

Can My Former Employer Deny My Unemployment?

Heck no. Fortunately, only your state can deny your unemployment. Although your former employer might tell them reasons why they think unemployment should be denied, it is the government that makes the final decision. If your state decides you aren't qualified, follow the instructions they send you to appeal. Here's some information that might help with your unemployment claim:

Misconduct: The standards are pretty high in most states for denying unemployment. Even though you can be fired at will, the employer usually must show deliberate misconduct on your part to convince the government you shouldn't get unemployment.

Quitting: If you resign for cause attributable to your employer (for example, sexual harassment, failure to pay wages, demotion, or wage reduction), you may still qualify for unemployment. If you quit because you didn't like the job, you probably won't qualify.

Working Long Enough: Most states have a set time you must have worked in order to qualify for unemployment. If you worked one job for 10 years, quit, and then get fired from another shortly after, you may not qualify even though you worked many years for the first one.

Release: Some states say it's illegal for employers to try to get you to release your unemployment. If you signed a release, you probably didn't give up your right to unemployment.

Donna's Tips

○ Apply as soon as you are fired or laid off. It takes a while to process your claim.

○ You won't get much money, but it's better than nothing while you're unemployed.

○ Some people think there's something wrong with collecting unemployment. It's your tax money. You should collect what you are entitled to when you need it.

○ Disclose all your income while you're collecting. If you withhold the fact that you earned wages while collecting, you may end up in jail.

The Company Offered My Job Back After I Complained. Should I Take It?

When I'm negotiating with employers to try to resolve employment issues, I almost always ask for reinstatement. Some people look at me in horror. "I don't want to go back there!" they cry. The truth about reinstatement is very few employers offer it. However, if you turn down reinstatement, you may lose some key rights. Here's what to think about if you're offered reinstatement:

Back Pay: By turning down reinstatement, you might lose your right to seek any further back pay if you have a case against the company. You'll almost certainly lose the right to front pay or future lost wages.

Retaliation: People worry about retaliation, but if you were fired for making a discrimination claim, complaining about unpaid wages, illegal activity of the company, or something similar, you may be legally protected against retaliation. If you're reinstated, you may want to have the company attorney or HR remind people of that. If you are retaliated against, report it immediately. If I've negotiated reinstatement, I usually request that non-retaliation be written into the agreement to avoid any confusion and remind people of their obligations.

Victory: Hold your head high when you return. Coworkers will probably have new respect for you. Don't run around saying how you beat the company, especially if you signed a confidentiality agreement.

Unsafe: If you're truly unsafe going back, such as where you've been physically assaulted or threatened with bodily harm and the person who did it is still there, by all means turn it down. Find out whether the harasser is still there, or has been fired or moved to a different location before you accept.

Same Conditions/Location: Verify, in writing, that you're being returned to the same job, same seniority, same conditions, same location, same hours—anything that's important to you. Otherwise you might end up working as a janitor on the night shift in another state.

Unemployment Discrimination: It's way easier to get a job if you have a job. You can always go back and start looking from a position of being employed. That way you can leave on your own terms when you're ready.

Donna's Tips

⊃ In this economy, if you don't have another job lined up and you aren't going to be in physical danger, take the job.

⊃ Don't go back to a job that is unsafe or has caused you to have a nervous breakdown. No potential case or job is worth your safety or sanity.

Crisis Scenarios for Your Post-Employment Issues

Scenario 1

You have access to your company's sales training and customer lists, and want to start your own business. You remember signing something about confidentiality when you started, but don't have a copy. Do you:

❑ a. Ask HR for a copy of all the contracts you signed, for your records? Read them carefully before you do anything.

❑ b. Copy it all onto a flash drive? Load it into your new business's computer. Make sure your new business is up and running with plenty of customers before you leave.

❑ c. Leave everything behind when you quit? Don't take any customer list or company materials. Turn in all copies of everything you have. If you use a company phone or laptop, turn it in when you leave. If you forwarded any company e-mails to your personal e-mail, erase them before you start your new business.

If you answered a:

If you think you can do this without alarming them, do it. Understand what you signed before you move on. Every state is different, so talk to a lawyer in your state if you have any questions.

If you answered b:

You'll probably spend years and tens of thousands of dollars defending yourself against a trade secret lawsuit.

If you answered c:

This is a good way to go. If you don't have a copy, assume you agreed to keep confidential materials confidential. Hopefully you didn't sign a non-compete provision you forgot about. Even so, some states allow you to compete as long as you don't use trade secrets or solicit company customers to do so.

Scenario 2

You start your own business. At a conference, a potential customer points to your former boss and says he is claiming you were fired for being incompetent. Do you:

❑ a. Walk across the room and punch your former boss in the face? Problem solved.

❑ b. Send a cease and desist letter to your former boss telling him to stop defaming you?

❑ c. Sue the bastard for tortious interference and defamation?

If you answered a:

I hope you enjoyed it. You'll have lots of time to laugh about it in jail.

If you answered b:

> This might work. Frequently if they find out you've caught them they'll stop. However, what he said may not be defamation.

If you answered c:

> If what he is saying is false and he is interfering with people who were ready to do business with you, you might have some claims against him. On the other hand, this might not cross any legal line. Watch him like a hawk and keep track of what he's saying about you, in case he does cross a line.

Scenario 3

Your boss makes blatant remarks about your religion. He fires you, saying he can't have someone working for him who has such stupid beliefs. Do you:

   ❑ a. Sue the bastards for religious discrimination?

   ❑ b. Complain to HR?

   ❑ c. File a charge of discrimination with the EEOC and your state agency?

If you answered a:

> You are going to have your suit dismissed. You failed to jump through the administrative hoops first.

If you answered b:

> With a situation this blatant, HR might actually intervene. However, even if they say they are going to help, you still must file your charge of discrimination timely. HR's actions won't stop the clock on your deadline.

If you answered c:

> You are taking the first step necessary before filing a suit for religious discrimination. You have preserved your right to sue. You must first file with the EEOC before you sue under Title VII. Your state probably has similar requirements.

Scenario 4

You have decided to start looking for another job. Your boss is pond scum and the company treats employees terribly. You want to keep working in the same industry. Do you:

❑ a. Keep working diligently for the company while you're looking? Don't copy or forward anything confidential.

❑ b. Copy all your contact information to take to the new company?

❑ c. Declare an in-cube sabbatical? Look like you're working, but surf the Internet for jobs instead.

If you answered a:

You are not only doing the classy thing, but you're meeting your legal requirements. If they're paying you to work, you must work and be loyal to the company while you're looking.

If you answered b:

If they are contacts you came in with, you may be entitled to them. If you signed a non-compete, non-solicitation, or confidentiality agreement, you may be getting yourself in trouble. Plus, even if you signed nothing, a confidential customer list might be a trade secret.

If you answered c:

You may be violating your duty of loyalty. If caught, you will be fired. Worse, they might even try to sue you for the wages you were paid while you weren't working.

Scenario 5

You signed a non-compete agreement when you started working. It says you can't work for a competitor for two years after you leave. Your company has a massive layoff. They announce they are closing your division and they are not going to be doing business in your industry anymore. Do you:

❑ a. Apply to industries that aren't competitors? Stay away from competitors for two years.

❑ b. Apply to competitors? If you get an offer, contact your company and tell them about it to see if they object.

❑ c. Don't worry about the non-compete? They can't enforce it. You have the right to work.

If you answered a:

You may be giving up unnecessarily. If they are abandoning your industry, they may not have a legitimate interest to protect. You may be able to fight the non-compete.

If you answered b:

This is the smart move. Don't sneak around. If they really are abandoning the industry, they might not care and give you their blessing. If
they say you can't work, go see a lawyer in your state to see if they can
knock some sense into your former employer. Abandoning the industry may be a defense to enforcement of your non-compete.

If you answered c:

You might get away with it. However, anyone who tells you that non-
competes aren't enforceable is an idiot. Talk to a lawyer in your state
to make sure of your rights. Being in a right to work state has zero to
do with your non-compete.

Scenario 6

You signed an employment agreement that includes a non-compete
provision. It also says what your salary is, as well as what your job duties
and benefits are. A few months after you start, you get a notice that your
pay is being cut and you are now the janitor. Do you:

❏ a. Quit and work for a competitor?

❏ b. Start a competing company?

❏ c. Take the janitor job? You can't afford not to work.

If you answered a:

You might be within your rights. If the agreement says it can only be
modified in writing signed by both parties and you didn't agree to the
pay cut and job change, they are in breach.

If you answered b:

Because they've breached, you may be okay. Just make sure you don't
take any company property or trade secrets when you leave.

If you answered c:

Whatever you do, don't sign a written modification agreeing to this.
If you must work, take it quietly while you're looking. If the cut is bad
enough, you might be better off on unemployment. In the meantime,
while you're looking elsewhere, talk to an employment lawyer in your
state about how to get out of the non-compete.

Scenario 7

You start a competing company and you are careful not to take anything confidential. You have a non-solicitation agreement saying you can't solicit your former employer's customers for a year after you leave. Without soliciting them, a customer tracks you down and says they want to follow you. Do you:

❑ a. Sign them up? Business is business.

❑ b. Tell them you'll be glad to talk to them in a year?

❑ c. Be careful what you say? They might be a spy for your old company.

If you answered a:

This may be okay. In some states, they can't stop a customer from voluntarily following you. However, that doesn't mean they won't sue anyway. You might have to spend tens of thousands of dollars (or more) proving you didn't solicit this customer.

If you answered b:

This is certainly the safe thing to do. You must decide whether this customer is worth the risk of litigation.

If you answered c:

You may be paranoid, but you're also smart. Many companies send friendly customers to new competitors to scope out the competition. Don't be surprised if you see an affidavit from this customer twisting everything you said.

Scenario 8

Shortly before you left the company, you forwarded a bunch of personal e-mails to yourself. You also burned a DVD with all your personal pictures on it. You then erased your personal e-mails and pictures. You get a letter from the company lawyer saying you stole trade secrets. They ask to have an expert inspect your computer at home. Do you:

❑ a. Ignore it? You don't work for them anymore.

❑ b. Erase everything you copied, and then talk to a lawyer?

❑ c. Let them inspect your computer? You have nothing to hide.

If you answered a:

You'll probably be sued. Ignoring a letter from a lawyer is like ignoring a letter from the IRS. Bad idea.

If you answered b:

By erasing everything, you look even more suspicious. It's not a bad idea to talk to a lawyer, but don't start deleting things. You probably have a duty to preserve any evidence. The expert will be able to tell you deleted things.

If you answered c:

Probably okay. However, if you really did copy company information, get some legal advice. Also, you might want to have a lawyer or your own expert oversee the operation so nothing gets planted on your computer.

Scenario 9

You go to work for a competing company. You don't remember signing any agreement with your former employer. The new boss gets a letter threatening to sue them if you aren't fired immediately. Your old company claims you signed a non-compete agreement. The new boss fires you. Do you:

- ❏ a. Ask the new boss for some time to resolve the matter? Go talk to a lawyer immediately.
- ❏ b. Sue the former employer for tortious interference with your employment?
- ❏ c. Ask for a copy of the non-compete you supposedly signed? Tell them that, if they fail to provide a copy, you'll assume you don't have one.

If you answered a:

You're being smart. Many times the new employer will give you some time to see if you can make the situation disappear. They don't want to be sued, but they want you.

If you answered b:

If you really don't have a non-compete, you might indeed have a claim against the company that cost you a job.

If you answered c:

Good idea. Give them a deadline and say if they don't produce it by then, you'll assume you don't have any such agreement. If they don't respond, go back to the new company and show them the letter. Ask for your job back. They might still want something in writing releasing you to work, but this is a good first step. If you did sign something, take it to a lawyer to review.

Scenario 10

When you are fired, your supervisor says: "Don't even bother to apply for unemployment. We always deny unemployment." Do you:

❑ a. Spend your time looking for a job instead of wasting your time?

❑ b. Apply anyway?

❑ c. Tell him that only the state can deny your unemployment? Then laugh openly in his face.

If you answered a:

Don't walk away from unemployment benefits based on an idle threat. They're benefits you earned.

If you answered b:

You probably know that only the state can deny your benefits. Although your former employer might challenge your entitlement, you have nothing to lose by applying and appealing if the benefits are denied.

If you answered c:

You've just ticked off someone unnecessarily. They'll probably challenge your unemployment for spite now. And forget about references. If they say this, don't respond. Just apply and do what you must do. Don't burn bridges.

Scenario 11

After you are fired, you file with the EEOC about the blatant discrimination you encountered. You get a call from HR offering your job back. Do you:

❑ a. Turn them down? You can't go back to someplace like that.

❑ b. Take it?

❑ c. Ask for specifics? Are you being returned to the same title? Same shift? Same location? Will the person who illegally harassed you still be your supervisor?

If you answered a:

You might have just cut off your right to recover any back pay from that date forward. You may even lose your unemployment. Unless the situation is dangerous, you should probably accept.

If you answered b:

In this economy, if you aren't already working, take the job. You can always start looking elsewhere. It's always easier to get a job if you have a job. If you are retaliated against, report it. You may be greeted by coworkers as a conquering hero, and many bullies don't dare mess with someone they know will fight back.

If you answered c:

You are being justifiably cautious. Sometimes it's a trick to get you to accept, and then make your life so miserable you quit. If the specifics are that it will be the same job, same benefits, and same shift, and that the harasser won't be your supervisor anymore (or has been disciplined and is under close watch), then take it.

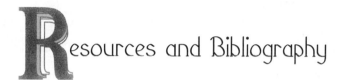

Resources and Bibliography

AUTHOR'S NOTE: Listed here are some key statutes and important Websites to give you a start. For a complete bibliography, including cases and secondary sources, please go to my Website: *www.donnaballman.com/files/Stand_Up_For_Yourself_Bibliography.pdf.*

Important Web Pages

United States Equal Employment Opportunity Commission, *www.eeoc.gov*

U.S. Department of Labor, *www.dol.gov*

National Employment Lawyers Association, *www.nela.org*

Internal Revenue Service, *www.irs.gov*

AFL-CIO, *www.aflcio.org*

OSHA, *www.osha.gov*

National Labor Relations Board, *www.nlrb.gov*

U.S. Department of Health and Human Services, *www.hhs.gov*

Society for Human Resource Management, *www.shrm.org*

U.S. Department of Justice, *www.justice.gov*

U.S. Securities and Exchange Commission, *www.sec.gov*

Statutes

Chapter 1

Fair Credit Reporting Act, 15 U.S.C.S. § 1681b

U.S. Bankruptcy Code, 11 U.S.C.S. § 525

Employee Polygraph Protection Act, 29 U.S.C.S. 2001, 29 C.F.R. § 801
Federal Arbitration Act, 9 U.S.C. § 1
Or. Rev. Stat. § 659A.030
Conn. Gen. Stat. § 46a-80
Ill. Com. Stat. Ann. § 5/2-103
Wis. Stat. § 111.321
18 Pa. Stat. § 9125
N.Y. Consol. Law. Serv. §752
Ks. Stat. § 22-4710
Haw. Rev. Stat. § 378-2
Ann. Laws Mass. Ch. 152, § 75B
Tex. Lab. Code § 451.001
85 Okla. Stat. § 5
Tenn. Code Ann. § 50-6-114

Chapter 2
EEO Regulations, 29 C.F.R. § 1614.105

Family and Medical Leave Act, 29 U.S.C.S. §§ 2611, 2619
Employee Retirement Income Security Act, 29 U.S.C. § 1001
Internal Revenue Code, 26 U.S.C. §§ 401, 3121
Consolidated Omnibus Budget Reconciliation Act, 29 U.S.C. § 1161
Health Insurance Portability and Accountability Act of 1996,
    42 U.S.C. § 1320d-2
Family and Medical Leave Act, 29 U.S.C. § 2611
FMLA Regulations, 29 C.F.R. 825.115
Americans with Disabilities Act of 1990, 42 U.S.C. § 12112
Health Insurance Portability and Accountability Act, 29 U.S.C. § 1181
National Labor Relations Act, 29 U.S.C. §§ 157, 164
Federal Railway Labor Act, 45 U.S.C. § 151
Taft-Hartley Act, 29 U.S.C. § 141
Electronic Communications Privacy Act, 18 U.S.C. § 2510
Fla. Stat. Ann. § 790.251
Ga. Code. Ann. § 16-11-135
Ind. Code Ann. § 34-28-7-2
26 Me. Rev. Stat. § 600
Haw. Rev. Stat. § 393-1
S.C. Code Ann. § 41-1-85
S.C. Code Ann. § 44-95-60
Me. Rev. Stat. Ann. tit. 22, § 1544
Minn. Stat. § 181.938

Wis. Stat. § 111.35
21 Vt. Stat. Ann. § 231
Wyo. Stat. Ann. § 27-9-105
Mont. Code Ann. §§ 39-2-901, 39-2-313

Chapter 3

Fair Labor Standards Act, 29 U.S.C. §§ 201, 203, 207, 213, 215, 216
FLSA Regulations, 29 C.F.R. §§ 541.200–541.302
FLSA Regulations, 29 C.F.R. §§ 785.18–785.19
OSHA Regulations, 29 C.F.R. § 1910.141
Affordable Care Act, 42 U.S.C. § 18001
Employee Retirement Income Security Act, 29 U.S.C. §§ 1181-1182
Uniform Services Employment and Reemployment Rights Act,
    38 U.S.C. §§ 4311-4312
Family and Medical Leave Act, 29 U.S.C. §§ 2611-2614
Americans with Disabilities Act of 1990, 42 U.S.C. § 12112
Electronics Communications Privacy Act of 1986, 18 U.S. §§ 2701, 2702
National Labor Relations Act, 29 U.S.C. § 157
Title VII, Civil Rights Act of 1964, 42 U.S.C. §§ 2000e–2000e-1
Age Discrimination in Employment Act, 29 U.S.C. § 630
Title VII, Civil Rights Act of 1964, 42 U.S.C. §§ 2000e–2000e-1
Age Discrimination in Employment Act, 29 U.S.C. § 630
Internal Revenue Code, 26 U.S.C. § 3121
Americans with Disabilities Act of 1990, 42 U.S.C. § 12112
FLSA Regulations, 29 C.F.R. §§ 541.200–541.302
Employee Retirement Income Security Act, 29 U.S.C. § 1001
National Labor Relations Act, 29 U.S.C. §§ 157, 164
Occupational Safety and Health Act, 29 U.S.C. § 660(c)
Surface Transportation Assistance Act, 49 U.S.C. § 31105
Asbestos Hazard Emergency Response Act, 15 U.S.C. § 2651
International Safe Container Act, 42 U.S.C. App. § 80507
Federal Rail Safety Act, 49 U.S.C. § 20109
National Transit Systems Security Act, 49 USC § 20109 Clean Air Act,
    42 U.S.C. § 7622
Energy Reorganization Act, 42 U.S.C. § 5851
Federal Water Pollution Control Act, 33 U.S.C. § 1367
Pipeline Safety Improvement Act, 49 USC § 60129
Safe Drinking Water Act, 42 U.S.C. § 300j-9(i)
Sarbanes-Oxley Act, 18 U.S.C. § 1514A
Solid Waste Disposal Act, 42 U.S.C. § 6971

Toxic Substances Control Act, 15 U.S.C. § 2622
Wendell H. Ford Aviation Investment and Reform Act, 49 U.S.C. § 42121
ct, 29 U.S.C. § 141
Haw. Rev. Stat. § 393
Mass. Gen. Laws ch. 111M, § 2
Mont. Code Ann. § 39-2-901
Ariz. Rev. Stat. § 23-1501(2)
Model Employment Termination Act, 7A U.L.A. §§ 80-99
Mass. Ann. Laws. ch. 149, § 185
Fla. Stat. Ann. § 92.57
Fla. Stat. Ann. § 772.11
Fla. Stat. Ann. § 832.05
Kan. Stat. Ann. § 21-3707
N.Y. Lab. Law § 198

Chapter 4
Uniformed Services Employment and Reemployment Rights Act of 1994, 38
U.S.C. §§ 4303, 4311
Family and Medical Leave Act, 29 U.S.C. § 2611
Fair Labor Standards Act, 29 U.S.C. §§ 203, 215
Age Discrimination in Employment Act, 29 U.S.C. § 630
Title VII, Civil Rights Act of 1964, 42 U.S.C. §§ 2000e–2000e-1, 2000e-3
National Labor Relations Act, 29 U.S.C. § 158
Fla. Stat. Ann. § 92.57
Or. Rev. Stat. § 659A.030
Rev. Code Wash. § 49.76.030

Chapter 5
Fair Labor Standards Act, 29 U.S.C. §§ 207, 213, 215
FLSA Regulations, 29 C.F.R. §§ 541.200–541.302, 541.602
Employee Retirement Income Security Act, 29 U.S.C. § 1132
Immigration Reform and Control Act, 8 U.S.C. § 1324a
Title VII, Civil Rights Act of 1964, 42 U.S.C. §§ 2000e–2000e-1
Age Discrimination in Employment Act, 29 U.S.C. § 630
Equal Pay Act, 29 U.S.C. § 206(d))
Family and Medical Leave Act, 29 U.S.C. § 2611
Consolidated Omnibus Budget Reconciliation Act, 29 U.S.C. § 1161
Civil Rights Act of 1871, 42 U.S.C. § 1983
Occupational Safety and Health Act, 29 U.S.C. § 660(c)
Sarbanes-Oxley Act, 18 U.S.C. §§ 1513, 1514A

Chapter 6

Title VII, Civil Rights Act of 1964, 42 U.S.C. §§ 2000e–2000e-5
Title VII Regulations, 29 C.F.R. § 1606.7
Age Discrimination in Employment Act, 29 U.S.C. §§ 623, 626, 630
Pregnancy Discrimination Act of 1978, 42 U.S.C. § 2000e(k)
Civil Rights Act of 1866, 42 U.S.C. §§ 1981, 1981a
Americans with Disabilities Act of 1990, 42 U.S.C. §§ 12101-12117
ADA Regulations, 29 C.F.R. § 1630.2
Genetic Nondiscrimination Act of 2008, 42 U.S.C. § 2000ff-1
Electronic Communications Privacy Act, 18 U.S.C. § 2511
Family and Medical Leave Act, 29 U.S.C. §§ 2611-2617
EEO Regulations, 29 C.F.R. § 1614.105
EEOC Regulations, 29 C.F.R. § 1605.1
Equal Pay Act, 29 U.S.C. § 206
Energy Reorganization Act, 42 U.S.C. § 5851
False Claims Act, 31 U.S.C. §§ 3730-3731
Statute of Limitations for Acts Arising from Acts of Congress,
    28 U.S.C. § 1658
Fair Labor Standards Act 29 U.S.C. § 215
Occupational Safety and Health Act, 29 U.S.C. § 660(c)
Surface Transportation Assistance Act, 49 U.S.C. § 31105
Asbestos Hazard Emergency Response Act, 15 U.S.C. § 2651
International Safe Container Act, 42 U.S.C. App. § 80507
Federal Rail Safety Act, 49 U.S.C. § 20109
National Transit Systems Security Act, 49 USC § 20109 Clean Air Act, 42
    U.S.C. § 7622
Energy Reorganization Act, 42 U.S.C. § 5851
Federal Water Pollution Control Act, 33 U.S.C. § 1367
Pipeline Safety Improvement Act, 49 USC § 60129
Safe Drinking Water Act, 42 U.S.C. § 300j-9(i)
Sarbanes-Oxley Act, 18 U.S.C. § 1514A
Solid Waste Disposal Act, 42 U.S.C. § 6971
Toxic Substances Control Act, 15 U.S.C. § 2622
Wendell H. Ford Aviation Investment and Reform Act, 49 U.S.C. § 42121
ct, 29 U.S.C. § 141
Comprehensive Environmental Response, Compensation, and Liability Act,
    42 U.S.C. § 9610
Consumer Product Safety Improvement Act, 15 U.S.C. § 2087
Affordable Care Act, 26 U.S.C. § 5000A
11 Del. Code § 2401

Fla. Stat. Ann. § 934.03
Fla. Stat. Ann. § 741.313
Miami-Dade County Ordinances § 11A-61
Massachusetts Executive Order No. 398
N.Y. Lab. Law § 10-b
O.R.C. § 4123.90
Iowa Code § 216.6
Mich. Code L. § 37.2202
Mont. Code Ann. § 39-2-901

Chapter 7

Consolidated Omnibus Budget Reconciliation Act (COBRA), 29 U.S.C. §§ 1161-1165
Employee Retirement Income Security Act (ERISA), 29 U.S.C. § 1001
Workers Adjustment and Retraining Notification Act (WARN), 29 U.S.C. §§ 2101-2104
22 Cal. Code Rev. § 1089-1
Fla. Stat. Ann. § 627.6692
N.M. Stat. Ann. § 50-12-1
Ariz. Rev. Stat. § 23-1361

Chapter 8

Montana: Mont. Code Ann. § 39-2-901
Fla. Stat. Ann. § 688.002
Fla. Stat. Ann. §§ 443.091, 443.101, 443.036, 443.041
Del. Code. § 3371
S.C. Code Ann. § 41-39-10

Index

About the Author

DONNA BALLMAN has been practicing employment law, including negotiating severance agreements and litigating discrimination, sexual harassment, non-compete agreements, and employment law issues in Ft. Lauderdale, Florida, since 1986. She is the award-winning author of *The Writer's Guide to the Courtroom: Let's Quill All the Lawyers,* a book geared toward informing novelists and screenwriters about the ins and outs of the civil justice system. Her blog on employee-side employment law issues, *Screw You Guys, I'm Going Home,* was named one of the 2011 ABA Blawg 100 and the 2011 Lexis/Nexis Top 25 Labor and Employment Law Blogs. She has written for *AOL Jobs, Monster.com, Ask a Manager,* and the *Huffington Post.* She has taught continuing legal education classes for lawyers and accountants through organizations such as the National Employment Lawyers Association, Sterling Education Services, and the Florida Association for Women Lawyers. She's been interviewed by MSNBC, the *Wall Street Journal,* Lifetime Television Network, the *Daily Business Review,* and many other media outlets on employment law issues. You can follow her on Twitter @EmployeeAtty.